CAUSE AND EFFECT
Intermediate Reading Practice

Patricia Ackert
University of Arizona
Center for English as a Second Language

illustrated by
Patricia Phelan Eisenberg

NEWBURY HOUSE PUBLISHERS, INC.
A Division of Harper & Row

Library of Congress Cataloging-in-Publication Data

Ackert, Patricia.
    Cause and effect.

    1. English language — Text-books for foreign speakers.
2. Readers — 1950-   . I. Title.
PE1128.A296   1986   428.6'4   86-12565
ISBN 0-88377-321-X

Cover by MGT Designs

Book design by Christy Rosso

Border art by Kathie Kelleher

NEWBURY HOUSE PUBLISHERS, INC.
A Division of Harper & Row

Language Science
Language Teaching
Language Learning

CAMBRIDGE, MASSACHUSETTS

Printed in the U.S.A.
63-20154

First printing: August 1986
2 4 6 8 10 9 7 5 3 1

CONTENTS

TO THE STUDENT

There are many advantages to learning English. One is that you can read information about thousands of subjects, because there is more information printed in English than in any other language. In this book you will read about some of the topics that are found in English language magazines, newspapers, and books. At the same time you will increase your knowledge of English.

TO THE INSTRUCTOR

This book is for students who know the basic structures of English and have a vocabulary of about 2000 English words. The 25 lessons are in five units. The exercises provide practice with vocabulary, comprehension, inference, main idea, cause and effect, context clues, scanning, sequence, summarizing, word forms, articles, prepositions, two-word verbs, compound words, connecting words, and noun substitutes.

An *Instructor's Manual* provides answers to all the exercises plus tests. There are unit tests which include a new reading selection with comprehension and main idea questions, general questions on the reading selections in the unit, and questions on the exercise material in the book. There are also short quizzes on the first two lessons for instructors who want to test their students during the first week. This manual may be obtained by writing to Newbury House Publishers, 54 Church Street, Cambridge, Massachusetts 02138.

Teaching Suggestions

The lessons in this book should be done in order because vocabulary is introduced gradually, repeated several times in the lesson where it first appears, and repeated in later lessons. Also, some of the exercises build to become more difficult; for example, the summary exercises start with selecting the sentence that best summarizes a paragraph and end with the students writing a summary of the whole reading selection.

I suggest that the instructor assign the reading text and some of the exercises for each lesson. For most of the exercises, the students can write the answers in the book and the instructor can go over them with the students in class, explaining or elaborating as necessary. At first, probably just the text, the vocabulary exercises, and possibly the comprehension and main idea exercises will be enough for one assignment. By the middle of the book the students should be able to do a whole lesson, or a little less if written work is assigned.

It has been my experience that most students need a lot of practice in writing. Because of this, I suggest that the comprehension questions be given as written assignments. The students should answer in complete sentences and use their own words as much as possible. If they do the exercises orally in class, they should make notes in the book and then give a complete sentence from the notes rather than reading the answer directly from the text.

Other exercises can also provide writing practice. The first few main idea and summary exercises are multiple choice, but then the students have to write their own sentences. One method of going over these exercises is for several students to put their sentences on the board and the class can then discuss which are best. However, this would probably be too time-consuming for the last unit where students write a summary of the whole text. The cause/effect and statement/reason exercises can be written assignments too.

It has also been my experience that students need a lot of practice using the context to understand new words. I suggest that when assigning a new lesson, the instructor save some class time to select sentences that clearly give the meaning of vocabulary items and have students tell what the words mean. The context clue exercises in the first two lessons teach the students how to do this.

Many of the vocabulary items are illustrated, glossed, or can be determined from the context. (Words in the text that are underlined are glossed or illustrated.) The context clue exercise also teaches vocabulary for the succeeding lesson. Most of the vocabulary is useful general vocabulary that the students should learn. The instructor should stress that the students must learn the vocabulary by the end of the lesson. The first lesson suggests that the students underline words they don't know and then test themselves when they finish the lesson.

I hope that the students will find the exercises useful in expanding their knowledge of the English language and that they will find the information as interesting as I did when I researched the book.

ACKNOWLEDGMENTS

I would like to thank several people for their help in writing this book. Chris Hasegawa, junior high school science teacher and CPR instructor for the American Heart Association, advised me on the science and CPR lessons. Dr. J.D. Garcia, physics professor at the University of Arizona, advised me on the photovoltaic lesson, and Dr. Leland Pederson, geography professor at the University of Arizona, helped me with the lesson on rain forests. Susan Ward from the UN Center in Tucson supplied materials and assistance for the lesson on *Women and Change*. Ellen Shepherd, M.Ed., C.G.A. and Walter Lindley, Program Coordinator for the Environmental Research Laboratory at the University of Arizona, were generous with their time and expertise for the two interview lessons. All of these people were most helpful in providing information and reviewing the lessons after I wrote them.

It has been a pleasure working with Jim Brown, editor at Newbury House, because he is a professional ESL teacher and writer as well as an editor. There should be more editors like him.

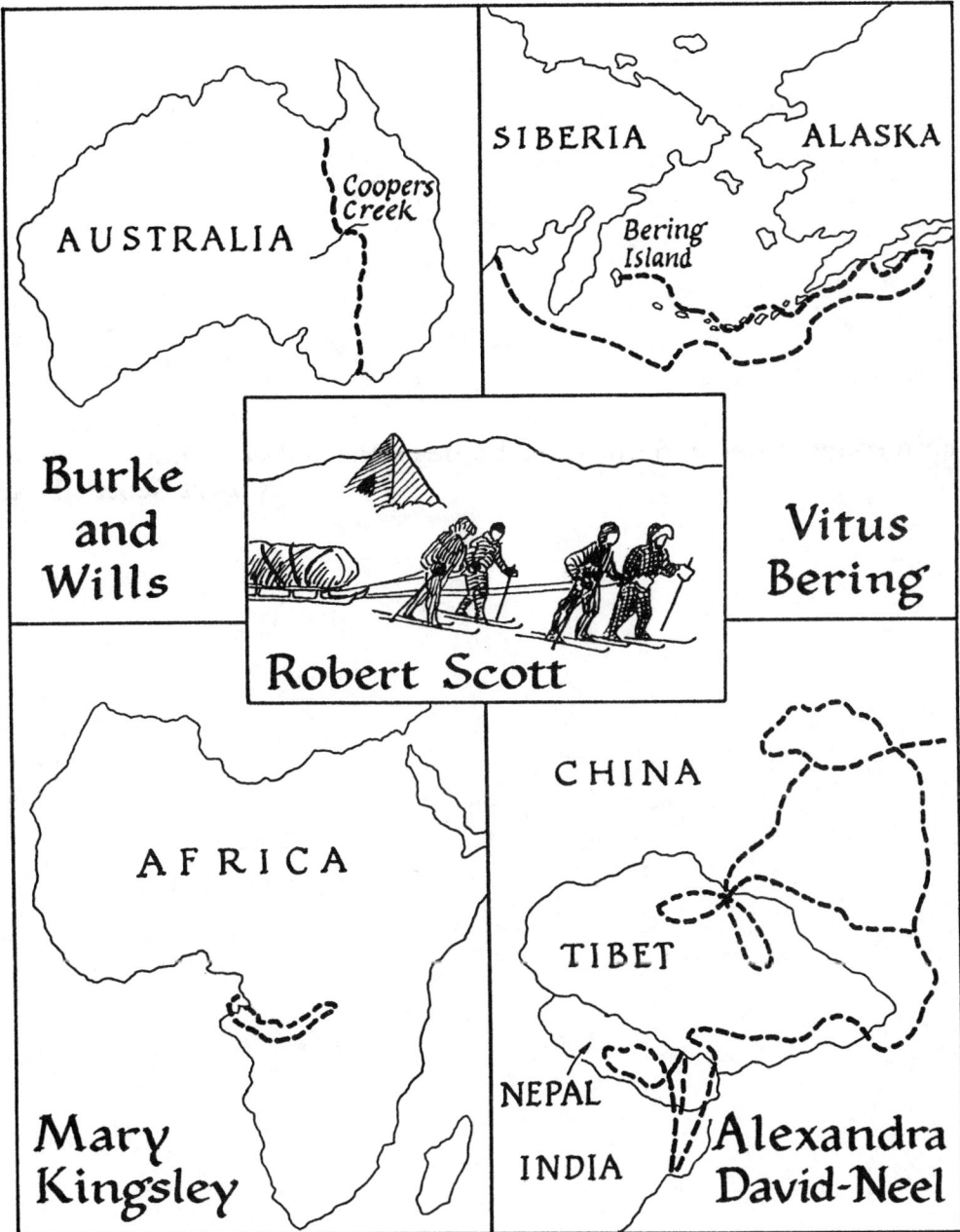

Unit I

EXPLORERS

AUSTRALIA

Coopers Creek

SIBERIA   ALASKA

Bering Island

Burke and Wills

Robert Scott

Vitus Bering

AFRICA

CHINA

TIBET

NEPAL

INDIA

Mary Kingsley

Alexandra David-Neel

These rough notes and our dead bodies must tell the tale.
—Robert Scott's Diary

BURKE AND WILLS— ACROSS AUSTRALIA

1

Australia is a **huge** country, and the outback (the Australian word for the interior of the country) is desert. Some years it rains only 8 centimeters in the outback, but other years rain-
5 storms **turn** the desert **into** sandy swamps.

very large

change into, become

Until the eighteenth **century**, only aborigines lived in Australia. These are tall, thin, brown-skinned people, the first people in Australia. When Europeans went there to live, they
10 built towns on the coast. However, by the 1850s, people began thinking more about the interior.

100 years

In 1860, Robert O'Hara Burke, a police officer from Ireland, was chosen to lead an expedition across the continent from south to
15 north. He took with him William John Wills and 11 other men, camels, horses, and enough supplies for a year and a half. They left Melbourne for the Gulf of Carpentaria on August 20, winter in the southern **hemisphere**.

half of the earth

20 The expedition had problems from the beginning. Burke had no experience in the outback. The men fought and would not follow orders. Twice they left some of their supplies so they could move faster, and later sent one of the
25 men, William Wright, back for them.

Finally, a small group led by Burke moved on ahead of the others to a river named Cooper's Creek and set up their base camp. They were

3

halfway across the continent, but it was summer
30 now, with very hot weather and sandstorms.

They waited for a month for Wright, and
then Burke decided that four from his small
group, with 3 months' supplies, should travel
the 1250 kilometers to the north coast as quickly
35 as possible. They told the others to wait for them
at Cooper's Creek.

The journey across the desert was very difficult, but at the end of January they reached the
Flinders River near the Gulf of Carpentaria.
40 They started their return journey, but now
it was the rainy season and traveling was slow
and even more difficult than their trip north.
They did not have enough food, and the men
became hungry and sick. Then one of them died.
45 Some of the camels died or were killed for food.

Finally, on April 21, they arrived back at
Cooper's Creek, only to find that no one was
there. The rest of the expedition left the day
before because they thought Burke must be
50 dead.

The three men continued south, but without enough food, both Burke and Wills died.
Aborigines helped the last man alive, and a
search party found him in September 1861. He
55 was half crazy from hunger and loneliness.

search = look for / party =
a group of people

There were many reasons that the expedition did not go as it was planned. It had an
inexperienced leader, the men made bad **deci-
sions**, some did not follow orders, and they did
60 not **get along**. But they were the first expedition to cross Australia, and Burke and Wills are
still known as heroes of exploration.

noun for decide
be friendly, not fight

EXPLORERS

A. Vocabulary

In this book, difficult words are repeated several times in the exercises. These words are also repeated and reviewed in other lessons. It is not necessary to list new English words with their meanings in your own language. You will learn them just by practicing. In each lesson, when you read the text the first time, underline the words that you don't know. Then you can give yourself a test when you finish the lesson. Look at the words you underlined and see if you understand them. If you don't know them yet, this is the time to memorize them.

In the vocabulary exercises in this book, write the correct word in each blank. Use each word only once. Use capital letters where they are necessary.

exploration	decision	hemisphere	experience
continents	ahead	expedition	century
aborigines	gets along	base	heroes

1. Please decide what you want to do. You must make a _____.
2. In baseball, a player hits the ball and runs to first _____.
3. The dark-skinned first Australians are called _____.
4. Do you have any _____ as a secretary, or is this your first job?
5. Kumiko _____ well with everyone. She is always nice and never fights with people.
6. The years 1900–1999 are the twentieth _____.
7. Tom saw some children _____ of him in the street while he was driving home, so he slowed down.
8. Asia is in the northern _____.
9. Africa, Antarctica, Asia, Australia, Europe, North America, and South America are the seven _____.
10. People who win in the Olympic Games are _____ in their countries.

B. Vocabulary

Do this exercise like Exercise A.

chosen	expedition	experience	exploration
huge	interior	journey	party
searching	supplies	swamps	turned into

1. Burke and Wills led an _____ into the interior of Australia.
2. Christopher Columbus was _____ for a new way to go to India.
3. Canada is a _____ country, one of the biggest in the world.
4. Birds like to live in _____ because there is a lot of water and food.
5. We use one kind of paint for the _____ of a house and another kind for the exterior.
6. It is a long _____ from Melbourne to London.
7. A search _____ was sent to find Burke and Wills' expedition.
8. Most of the earth has been explored. Now we are in the age of space _____, searching for more information about the stars, the moon, and other planets besides earth.
9. The secretary ordered paper, pens, and other _____ for the office.
10. Carlos started to study hard and _____ a good student.

C. True/False

Write **T** if the sentence is true. Write **F** if it is false. If a question is false, change it to make it true, or explain why it is false.

An asterisk(*) before a question means it is either an **inference** or an **opinion** question. You cannot find a sentence in the text with the answer. You have to use the information in the text and things you already know and then decide on the answer.

_____ 1. The first Europeans in Australia built villages in the outback because there were too many aborigines on the coast.

_____ 2. The Burke and Wills expedition crossed Australia from south to north.

_____ *3. December is a summer month in Australia.

_____ 4. Much of the interior of Australia is swampy all year long.

_____ 5. Eleven men crossed Australia with Burke and Wills.

_____ *6. Burke and Wills did not have enough food for their journey back to Cooper's Creek because the rain slowed them down.

_____ *7. The aborigines could help the last man alive because they understood how to live in the desert.

_____ 8. Burke was a good leader for this expedition.

D. Comprehension Questions

Answer these questions in complete sentences. An asterisk(*) means it is either an **inference** or an **opinion** question. You cannot find the exact answer in the text.

1. Where did the first Europeans live when they went to Australia?
*2. Why were camels good animals for this expedition?
3. Why did the men leave some of their supplies behind them?
4. Why was it difficult to travel in the interior of Australia?
5. What happened to some of the camels?
6. Name two reasons why this expedition had so many problems.
*7. Do you think Burke and Wills should be called heroes of exploration? Why?

E. Main Idea

What is the main idea of paragraph 4 (lines 20–25)?

1. Robert Burke led this expedition.
2. The expedition had many problems.
3. Burke had no experience in the outback.

8

8

WORD STUDY

A. Two-Word Verbs

English has many two-word verbs. Each of the two words is easy, but when they are put together, they mean something different. There is often no way to guess what they mean. You have to learn each one. Learn these and then fill in the blanks with the right words. Use the right verb form.

turn into — change into, become
get along (with) — not fight, be friendly
break down — stop going or working (often about a car)
call on — when someone, usually a teacher, asks someone to speak
put away — put something in the place it belongs

1. Our washing machine _____ yesterday and I couldn't finish washing my clothes.
2. Tommy and his little brother don't _____ very well. They fight about something almost every day.
3. Ali knew the answer when the teacher _____ him.
4. It was rainy this morning, but now it has _____ a beautiful day.
5. Mary doesn't usually _____ her clothes. She just leaves them on a chair or the bed.

B. Articles (a, an, the)

There are so many rules about articles that it is easier just to get used to them by practicing than to learn all the rules. However, you will learn a few of the rules later in this book. Here are some sentences or parts of sentences from the text. Put an article in the blank if it is necessary.

1. Other years rainstorms turn _____ desert into sandy swamps.
2. Until _____ eighteenth century, only aborigines lived in _____ Australia.
3. In 1860, _____ Robert O'Hara Burke, _____ police officer from Ireland, was chosen to lead _____ expedition across _____ continent from south to north.
4. He took with him William John Wills, _____ eleven other men, _____ camels, _____ horses, and enough supplies for _____ year and _____ half.

5. _____ expedition had _____ problems from _____ beginning.
6. _____ men fought and would not follow _____ orders.

C. Context Clues

It is not necessary to look up every new word in the dictionary. You can often tell what the word means from the sentence it is in, or from the sentence after it. For example, the word **aborigines** in line 6 is explained in the next sentence. What are aborigines?

Always look for this kind of sentence when you are reading. Don't look up the word in your dictionary.

Here are some sentences from the other four lessons in this unit. Tell what each word in **bold** print means.

1. She started working as a **journalist**, writing articles about Asia and Buddhism for English and French magazines and newspapers.
2. Scott took **ponies** (small horses) and a few dogs.
3. She helped to start **anthropology**, the study of people's customs and lives, in Africa.
4. Europeans bought **ivory**, which comes from elephants, and other things from Africans.
5. She met **traders** there, European men who bought ivory and other things from Africans and sold them things from Europe.
6. **Missionaries** went to Africa to teach Christianity.

ALEXANDRA DAVID-NEEL — A FRENCH WOMAN IN TIBET

2

Tibet has been a secret and mysterious country to the rest of the world for several centuries. It is on a high **plateau** in Asia, surrounded by even higher mountains, and only a
5 few foreigners were able to cross its **borders** until recently.

One of these foreigners was a French woman named Alexandra David-Neel (1868–1969). She traveled by herself in India, China,
10 and Tibet. She studied the Buddhist religion, wrote articles and books about it, and collected **ancient** Buddhist books. She also became a Buddhist herself.

Alexandra always said she had an unhappy
15 childhood. She **escaped** her unhappiness by reading books on adventure and travel. She ran away from school several times and even ran away to England when she was only sixteen.

She was a singer for several years, but in
20 1903 she started working as a journalist, writing articles about Asia and Buddhism for English and French magazines and newspapers. The next year, when she was thirty-seven, she married Philippe-François Neel. It was a strange
25 marriage. After five days together, they moved to different cities and never lived together again.

high, flat land

lines between countries

very old

got away from

10

Yet he **supported** her all his life, and she wrote him hundreds of letters full of details about her travels.

yet = but / supported =
gave her money to live on

30 She traveled all over Europe and North Africa, but she went to India in 1911 to study Buddhism, and then her real travels began. She traveled in India and in Nepal and Sikkim, the small countries north of India in the Himalaya

35 Mountains, but her goal was Tibet. She continued to study Buddhism and learned to speak Tibetan. She traveled to villages and religious centers, with only an interpreter and a few men to carry her camping equipment. For several

40 months she lived in a **cave** in Sikkim and studied Buddhism and the Tibetan language. Then she adopted a fifteen-year-old Sikkimese boy to travel with her. He remained with her until his death at the age of fifty-five.

45 For the next 7 years she traveled in remote areas of China. These were years of civil war in China, and she was often in danger. She traveled for thousands of kilometers on horseback with a few men to help her, through desert heat, sand-

50 storms, and the rain, snow, and **freezing** temperatures of the colder areas.

0°C or colder

In 1924, David-Neel was fifty-six years old. She darkened her skin and dressed as an old **beggar**. She carried only a beggar's bowl and a

55 backpack and traveled through hot lowlands and snowy mountain passes until she reached the border of Tibet. Because she spoke Tibetan so well, she was able to cross the border and reach the famous city of Lhasa without anyone know-

60 ing that she was European and **forbidden** to be there. It was often freezing cold, and sometimes there wasn't enough food. Sometimes she was sick, and once she nearly died. This was the most dangerous of all her journeys, but she reached

65 her goal and collected more information about Tibetan Buddhism.

not allowed

She returned to France in 1925. She spent several years writing about her **research** and adventures and translating ancient Tibetan re-
70 ligious books. When she was sixty-six, she returned to China and the Tibetan border area for 10 years. In 1944, the Second World War reached even that remote area, and at the age of seventy-six she walked for days, sometimes
75 without food, until she was able to reach a place where she could fly to India and then home to France. She continued writing and translating until she died, just 7 weeks before her 101st birthday.
80 Most explorers traveled to discover and map new places. David-Neel went to do research on Buddhism. She said that freedom was the most important thing in life for her, and like many other explorers, she lived a dangerous,
85 exciting, free life.

search for new information

A. Vocabulary
Write the correct word in each blank. Use each word only once and use capital letters if they are necessary.

civil war	temperature	freezes	border
mysterious	article	ancient	discovered
caves	journalist	remote	forbidden
equipment	adventure	beggars	plateau

1. It would be a great _____ to travel in Tibet on horseback.
2. There is an interesting _____ in the newspaper today about Tibet.
3. You can find _____ asking for money in most countries.
4. When Ali got to his car, he _____ that he had a parking ticket.
5. Some ancient North American Indians lived in _____. Others built houses.
6. Smoking is _____ in the front rows in airplanes.

7. When water _____, it turns into ice.
8. Did you bring all the sports _____ for our picnic?
9. The Himalayas are on the _____ between China and India.
10. A _____ collects information and then writes articles about it for magazines and newspapers.
11. The language of _____ Egypt was different from the modern Egyptian language.
12. The United States had a _____ between the northern and southern states from 1861 to 1865.

B. Vocabulary

Remember to underline the words you don't know as you read the text and then test yourself when you finish the lesson.

plateau	escaped	area	mysterious
details	surrounded	support	journalist
yet	research	border	religion
adopted	temperature	remote	frozen

1. It's hot today. What is the _____?
2. Northern Siberia is _____ from Russian cities.
3. A _____ noise woke me up in the middle of the night.
4. Mr. and Mrs. Thompson _____ a baby because they couldn't have any children of their own.
5. What is your _____? Are you a Christian?
6. Most English paragraphs have a main idea and supporting _____.
7. Parents usually _____ their children until the children finish school. The parents pay for everything the children need.
8. Dr. Garcia is doing _____ for space exploration.
9. Tibet is a remote country, _____ tourists go there now.
10. A man _____ from prison last night. He is dangerous.
11. Our house is _____ by big trees.
12. Tibet is on a _____ north of the Himalayas.
13. There are a lot of apartment buildings in the _____ around the university.

C. Multiple Choice

Circle the letter of the best answer. An asterisk (*) means it is an inference or opinion question, and you cannot find the answer in a sentence in the text.

1. Alexandra David-Neel went to Asia to _____.
   a. study Buddhism
   b. lead an expedition
   c. adopt a son

2. When she was a child, she read to _____.
   a. become a Buddhist
   b. escape her unhappiness
   c. learn about Europe

3. After she got married, _____.
   a. she lived in Europe with her husband for several years
   b. her husband supported her
   c. her husband traveled in Europe with her

*4. It is possible that she _____.
   a. took photographs during her travels
   b. had a car when she lived in a cave
   c. spoke Tibetan to her Indian friends

5. The country she wanted most to visit was _____.
   a. India
   b. China
   c. Tibet

6. Her travels in China were dangerous because _____.
   a. there was a civil war
   b. she was traveling on horseback
   c. she was a beggar

7. David-Neel said that _____.
   a. she wasn't afraid of danger
   b. freedom was very important to her
   c. she wanted her husband to travel with her

D. Comprehension Questions
Always answer the comprehension questions with complete sentences.

1. Why is Tibet a mysterious country?
*2. Why did Alexandra run away from school?
3. What is a journalist?
4. Why was her marriage strange?
5. What did she do when she was living in a cave?
6. What does *remote areas* mean?
7. Why didn't the Tibetans know she was a foreigner?
8. What kind of work did she do after her last trip?
*9. Do you think she lived a free life? Why?

E. Main Idea
What is the main idea of paragraph 3 (lines 14–18)?

1. Alexandra read books on travel and adventure.
2. Alexandra ran away from school several times.
3. Alexandra had an unhappy childhood.

WORD STUDY

A. Word Forms

Choose the right word form for each sentence. Use a word from line 1 in sentence 1, and so on. Use the right verb forms and singular or plural nouns.

	Verb	Noun	Adjective	Adverb
1.	mystify	mystery	mysterious	mysteriously
2.	surround	surroundings		
3.	beg	beggar		
4.		religion	religious	religiously
5.		adventure	adventurous	adventurously
6.	supply	supply		
7.	equip	equipment		
8.	adopt	adoption		
9.	discover	discovery		
10.	decide	decision		decidedly

1. I saw an exciting television program last night. It was a _____.
2. Dan drove so fast on his vacation trip that he hardly saw his _____.
3. Small children often _____ to go with their parents when the parents go out at night.
4. Alexandra David-Neel was a very _____ woman.
5. David-Neel was also very _____.
6. The company was unable to _____ most of the things we ordered.
7. The Browns are going to _____ their truck with a telephone.
8. It is very difficult to _____ children in the United States today.
9. Captain James Cook is famous for the _____ of many Pacific islands.
10a. Sometimes it is difficult to make a good _____ on a difficult problem.
10b. David-Neel was a _____ adventurous woman. There is no question about it.

B. Articles

A and **an** are used to show that the noun after it is one of a group.

John Burke was **an** explorer. (He was one of all the explorers in history.)
Maria is **a** student. (She is one of all the students in the world.)
There is **an** apple in the refrigerator. (This is one of all the apples in the world.)

The is used to show the noun is one special, particular, specific noun or nouns.

John Burke and William John Wills were **the** first explorers to cross Australia.
Maria is **the** best student in the class.
There is an apple in **the** refrigerator. (We know that we are talking about the refrigerator in our kitchen.)

Put the right article in the blanks.

1. Australia is _____ huge country.
2. The USSR is _____ largest country in the world in area.
3. _____ journalist who wrote this article is a friend of mine.
4. David-Neel was _____ journalist.
5. Would you please close _____ door?
6. Her office is _____ first one on the left.
7. _____ professor called you today, but I don't know who it was.
8. Who was _____ worst teacher you ever had?

C. Compound Words

Compound words are common in English. They are two words put together, and the meaning of the compound word is related to the meaning of the two words. They are not like two-word verbs where the meaning is different from the meaning of each word by itself.

Put these compound words in the right blanks.

horseback	sandstorm	snowstorm	keyhole
mailbox	sidewalk	doorbell	weekend

1. Barbara couldn't drive to her parents' last week because there was a bad _____ and it was very cold.

2. Abdullah looks in his _____ every day and he usually finds a letter.

3. A _____ is a place for people to walk at the side of the street.

4. When you unlock a door, you put your key in the _____ .

5. The _____ rang, and Susan went to answer the door.

6. Did you ever go _____ riding?

D. Context Clues

You can often guess the meaning of a word from the sentence even if the sentence doesn't explain the word exactly. For example, in the next lesson, a sentence says "They lost a lot of their food when one of the ships **sank** in a storm." What could a storm do to a ship so that the food was lost? The ship probably went down into the water to the bottom of the ocean. When you can guess easily what the word means from the sentence, don't look up the word in your dictionary.

Now practice with these new words from the next lessons. Circle the letter of the best meaning of the **bold** word.

1. Please write your **complete** name, not just your family name.
   a. first   b. whole   c. first and last

2. David-Neel had to go to China first **in order to** go to Tibet.
   a. to   b. by   c. for

3. This book **includes** lessons on explorers, science, and medicine.
   a. has in it
   b. has complete information
   c. has only

4. On my last flight to London, there was a **delay** of three hours because of bad weather. I waited in an airport restaurant.
   a. danger   b. line   c. wait

5. After three weeks at sea, the sailors were happy to go **ashore** in Singapore.
   a. for the weekend   b. to the land   c. swimming

6. After the **decade** of 1990–1999, it will be the twenty-first century.
   a. 100 years   b. 10 years   c. 50 years

VITUS BERING – ACROSS SIBERIA TO NORTH AMERICA

3

In 1733, the most complete scientific expedition in history up to that time left St. Petersburg (now called Leningrad), Russia, to explore the east coast of Siberia and discover if Asia and
5 North America were joined. The scientists planned to report on everything: the geography, climate, plants, and animals, and the customs and languages of the Siberian people.

The expedition had to cross Siberia **in**
10 **order to** reach the Pacific Ocean. Vitus Bering,   to
the leader of the whole expedition, left St. Petersburg with almost 600 people. The group
included a few scientists, skilled workers of all   had in it
kinds, soldiers, and sailors. Alexei Chirikov left
15 later with most of the scientists and tons of supplies.

It took 7 years for Bering's and Chirikov's groups to cross Siberia. They traveled mostly in flat-bottomed boats on the rivers. Bering's group
20 spent a year in Tobolsk where they built a ship and explored the Ob River. They continued to Yakutsk where they spent 4 years. Yakutsk was only a small village, so they had to build their own buildings because there were so many
25 people in the expedition. They also built boats and explored the Lena River. Then they moved on to Okhotsk on the eastern coast. It took two

more years to build ships so they could explore
and map the east coast.

30   Bering made careful plans, but there were
always problems. For example, they lost a lot of
their food when one of the ships **sank** in a storm.
But finally, their two ships started for North
America. They had only one summer instead of
35 two years for their explorations because of the
many problems and delays. And summers are
short in the north.

went to the bottom of
the ocean

There was more bad luck. There were
storms, and the two ships were **separated**, but
40 at last the sailors on Bering's ship saw mountains a short distance across the sea. This proved
that North America and Asia were two separate
continents.

moved apart

Their problems continued. Their water sup-
45 ply was low, but when the men went ashore in
Alaska, they got water that was a little salty.
Many of the men were sick from scurvy, a disease caused by the **lack** of vitamin C. When they
drank the salty water, they became even sicker.
50 Then they started dying, one after another.

not enough of or none

As the ship sailed south, back toward Okhotsk, it became lost in storms. Finally, a storm
drove it onto a small island, and the men knew
their ship could not sail again. They were in a
55 place with no trees, but there were birds and
animals for food, and fresh water to drink. However, it was too late for many of them. Men
continued to die from scurvy, and on December
8, 1741, Bering died and was buried on the island
60 which is now named for him. When spring came,
the few remaining men were able to build a small
ship from the wood in the old one and leave the
island.

By this time, the Russian government had
65 lost interest in the North Pacific. Bering's
reports were sent back to St. Petersburg and
forgotten. **Decades** later, people realized that

one decade = ten years

EXPLORERS

Bering was a great explorer. His expedition gathered important scientific information about the
70 interior of Siberia, made maps of the eastern coast, and discovered a new part of North America. Today we have the Bering Sea between Siberia and Alaska to **remind us** of the leader of this great scientific expedition.

make us remember

A. Vocabulary

complete	realize	included	delay
distance	bury	gather	history
remind	sink	separate	lack

1. They could see something in the _____, but they couldn't tell what it was.
2. Did you study the _____ of your country in school?
3. Mr. and Mrs. Baker drive to work in _____ cars because they work in different places.
4. Please _____ me to buy some bread, or I might forget.
5. In some restaurants, the waiter's tip is _____ in the bill. In others you leave it separately.
6. You should do the _____ lesson for tomorrow's homework. Do all the exercises.
7. There will be a short _____ while the chemistry professor gets the equipment ready.
8. He didn't _____ what time it was, and he got to class late.
9. Wood doesn't _____ in water. Rocks do.
10. Burke's expedition failed partly because of his _____ of experience in the Australian outback.

B. Vocabulary

climate	in order to	bury	gathered
custom	ashore	fresh	skilled
complete	decade	vitamin	scurvy

1. Ali is studying English _____ go to an American university.
2. In many countries it is the _____ to _____ people when they die.
3. Ann _____ up her books and papers and left the library.
4. _____, caused by the lack of vitamin C, was a problem on ships on long trips.
5. North Africa has a desert _____.
6. A century is 100 years. A _____ is 10.
7. Electricians and mechanics are _____ workers.
8. After a half hour in the water, the children swam _____ and dried off.
9. People cannot drink sea water. They need _____ water.
10. _____ C is found in oranges.

C. Vocabulary Review: Definitions
Match the words with their meaning.

1. hemisphere _____
2. border _____
3. forbidden _____
4. get along _____
5. research _____
6. plateau _____
7. discover _____
8. ancient _____
9. turn into _____
10. journalist _____

a. not fight
b. find
c. high flat land
d. inside
e. half of the earth
f. not allowed
g. 100 years
h. writer for magazines
i. search for new information
j. very old
k. become
l. line between two countries

D. True/False

Write **T** if the sentence is true, **F** if it is false, and **NI** if there is no information in the text. Change the false sentences to make them true, or explain why they are false.

_____   1. Bering left St. Petersburg ahead of Chirikov.
_____   2. It took them 7 years to cross Siberia because they were traveling on horseback.
_____   3. Vitus Bering was from St. Petersburg.
_____   4. Bering spent 2 years exploring the east coast of Siberia.
_____   *5. Bering's and Burke's expeditions were similar.
_____   6. Bering's men found Eskimos in Alaska.
_____   7. Scurvy is caused by a lack of vitamin C.
_____   8. Alaska belonged to the United States at the time of Bering's expedition.

E. Comprehension Questions

Try to answer the comprehension questions in your own words instead of using the exact words from the text.

1. Why was this called a scientific expedition?
2. What did the men on the expedition do in Tobolsk?
3. Where did they stay longer, in Tobolsk or Yakutsk?
*4. Why did the expedition have to build boats?
5. How did the two ships get separated in the Pacific Ocean?
6. Why did the men on the island continue to die even when they had food and water?
*7. Is scurvy a problem on ships today? Why or why not?
*8. When Bering's expedition returned to St. Petersburg, were they welcomed as national heroes? Why or why not?

F. Main Idea

What is the main idea of paragraph 3 (lines 17–29)?

1. It took 7 years to cross Siberia.
2. The expedition explored two rivers.
3. The expedition built their own village in Yakutsk.

WORD STUDY

A. Reading

How carefully should you read? How fast should you read? These questions have different answers. Sometimes you have to read slowly and carefully. Other times you read fast, and other times you read at a regular speed.

How would you read these things? Use these answers:

    a. slowly and carefully   b. at a regular speed   c. fast

(Students may have different answers.)

1. a letter from your parents
2. the text of these lessons
3. the homework for a difficult science class
4. the newspaper
5. a magazine article on an interesting person
6. an exciting mystery story

     Some students like to read a whole text quickly for the general idea. Others like to start at the beginning and read each sentence carefully. You can choose the best way for you to start reading a lesson. After that, probably you need to read the lesson two or three times. When you come to a word you don't know, read the sentence again, or even three times, to help you remember the word. It is never necessary to memorize sentences or paragraphs. This is not the way to study reading.

     If the text is very difficult for you, read the first paragraph two or three times, then the second, and so on. Then read the whole text from beginning to end. Then you might want to read it all again.

     You will probably want to read the complete text again after you have finished the whole lesson. Then test yourself on the vocabulary words that you underlined when you first read the text and learn the words you don't know.

B. Word Forms: Verbs

How do you know which form of a word to use? This information will help you.

     Every sentence must have a verb. There are often clues that tell you what form of the verb to use.

EXPLORERS

Put the right verb form in these blanks. Explain why you chose each form.

(lead)   1. Did Bering _____ an expedition across Siberia?
(leave)   2. The expedition _____ St. Petersburg in 1733.
(study)   3. Bob is _____ about explorers.
(learn)   4. Nadia has _____ a lot of words this week.
(help)   5. Can you _____ me with this exercise?
(give)   6. The teacher _____ a lot of homework every day.
(sleep)   7. Mr. Gorder was _____ at midnight last night.
(travel) 8. They are going to _____ in Europe next summer.

C. Prepositions

Prepositions are difficult. The best way to learn how to use the right preposition is by practicing. Write the prepositions in these sentences from the text.

1. _____ 1733, the most complete scientific expedition in history _____ _____ that time left St. Petersburg.
2. The scientists planned to report _____ everything.
3. The expedition had to cross Siberia _____ order to reach the Pacific Ocean.
4. Vitus Bering, the leader _____ the whole expedition, left St. Petersburg _____ almost 600 people.
5. They traveled mostly _____ flat-bottomed boats _____ the rivers.
6. They had only one summer instead _____ two years _____ their explorations because _____ the many problems and delays.
7. At last the sailors _____ Bering's ship saw mountains a short distance _____ the sea.
8. They were _____ a place _____ no trees, but there were birds and animals _____ food.
9. _____ this time, the Russian government had lost interest _____ the North Pacific.
10. It discovered a new part _____ North America.

D. Context Clues

The words in the Context Clues exercises are always words in the next lesson. Circle the letter of the right answer.

1. Isamu's English is not very good. He **frequently** makes mistakes.
   a. quickly   b. often   c. never

2. Oil, gas, and wood are all kinds of **fuel**.
   a. something to burn for heat
   b. something to make cars go
   c. something to build ships from

3. David-Neel walked for days when she was seventy-six years old. She was often **exhausted**.
   a. very hungry   b. very tired   c. very old

4. Jean was in an automobile accident and **injured** her leg.
   a. hurt   b. stepped on   c. stood on

5. **At times** Neel became sick from the food she ate.
   a. usually   b. sometimes   c. at different hours

6. Burke's expedition had **terrible** problems and several men died.
   a. large   b. interesting   c. very bad

7. We know about Burke's expedition because he wrote in a **diary** every day. The search party found it.
   a. a notebook about what happened every day
   b. a cassette recording about what happened every day
   c. a book about a person's life

ROBERT SCOTT – A RACE TO THE SOUTH POLE

4

Roald Amundsen, a Norwegian, was the first person to reach the South Pole. Robert Scott, an Englishman, arrived at the South Pole a month after Amundsen and died on the return
5 journey to his ship. Yet, strangely enough, Scott became a hero and Amundsen did not.

Captain Robert Scott (1868–1912) was an English Navy officer. He led an expedition to Antarctica in 1901–1904 for a British scientific
10 organization called the Royal Geographical Society. His group traveled farther south than anyone else had ever done, and he gathered information on rocks, the weather, and climate, and made maps. When he returned to England, he
15 was a national hero.

A few years later he decided to organize another expedition. He said he wanted to make a complete scientific study of Antarctica, but he really wanted to be the first person at the South
20 Pole. He took three doctors, several scientists, and other men with him.

They sailed on a ship named the *Terra Nova* in June 1910, but when they reached Australia, they learned that Amundsen was also on his way
25 to the Pole.

Amundsen and Scott were very different from each other and made very different plans. Amundsen planned everything very carefully.

He took sleds and dog teams as the great Arctic
30 explorers did. Scott took ponies (small horses),
and a few dogs, but he planned to have his men
pull the sleds themselves for most of the trip. On
other expeditions, as some dogs became weak,
the men killed them for food for themselves and
35 the other dogs. Amundsen did this too, and it
helped him reach the Pole, but later people
called him "dog eater." Scott would not eat dogs,
and this was one reason he died on this expedition.

40   There were other differences between the
two expeditions. Amundsen sailed 100 kilometers closer to the Pole than Scott did. Scott also
had the bad luck of having very bad weather —
days of **blizzards** and strong winds. It was often   storm with wind and snow
45 − 40°C (minus 40 degrees Celsius).

    Scott and his men built a building as their
base camp near the ocean's edge and spent the
winter there. They used sleds and ponies to carry
a ton of supplies farther **inland** to a place that   toward the interior
50 they named the One Ton Depot. When spring
came, a few of the men started ahead of the
others with motorized sleds to leave supplies
along the way. However, after only a few days
the sleds broke down and the men had to pull
55 them.

    A few days later Scott started for the South
Pole with a few men. The whole journey was
very difficult. Scott and his men either walked
and skied through deep snow or over ice and
60 uneven ground. The climate was too difficult
for the ponies and they all died. There were
frequent snowstorms. Sometimes the men   often
couldn't leave their tents for several days because of blizzards.

65   When Scott was 260 kilometers from the
Pole, he sent all but four men back to the base
camp. This was probably his most serious mistake. He had a tent big enough for four people

and only enough food and fuel for four, but now
70 there were five. Also, one man had left his skis
behind with some of the supplies. He had to walk
in the snow, and this slowed down the whole
group.

On January 17, 1912, Scott and his men
75 reached the Pole, only to find a tent and the
Norwegian flag. They were not the first people to
reach the South Pole. They had lost the race.

The next day they started the 1300-kilo-
meter journey back to their base camp, pulling
80 their heavy sleds full of supplies. The trip back
was worse than on their way to the Pole. They
became weak from hunger. **At times** the white-   sometimes
ness everywhere made them blind. Their fingers
and toes began to freeze and two of the men fell
85 and **injured** themselves. They never had   hurt
enough fuel to keep warm in their tent. They
became **exhausted**, and it was more and more   very tired
difficult to pull the sleds.

Finally, one man died. Then another be-
90 came so weak that he knew he was endangering
the lives of the others. One night he left the tent
and never returned. He walked out into the
blizzard and died instead of holding back the
other three.

95 Every day Scott described the terrible journey in his diary. On March 21 the three remaining men were only 20 kilometers from the One
Ton Depot, but another blizzard kept them in
their tent. On March 29 they were still unable to
100 leave their tent. On that day, Scott wrote his last
words in his diary.

A search party found the three bodies 8
months later. They also found Scott's diary, excellent photographs of the expedition, and let-
105 ters to take back to England. The search party
left the frozen bodies where they found them.

Today the building at the base camp is still
there. Inside there are supplies, furniture, and

things that belonged to the men. They are left
110 just the way they were when Scott's expedition
was there. New Zealand takes care of the building and its contents.

Robert Scott's name lives on as a great
explorer of Antarctica, the last part of the earth
115 that people explored. He was not the first to
reach the South Pole, and he and his men died
because of his bad planning, but he is remem-
bered as one of the great heroes of exploration.

A. Vocabulary

organization	each other	sleds	inland
pony	blizzard	break down	exhausted
blind	frequent	fuel	at times

1. A _____ is a storm with wind and snow.
2. Scott and his men slept close to _____ in a small tent.
3. A _____ is a small horse, not a young horse.
4. People who grow up near the sea are often unhappy if they have to move
   _____.
5. A _____ person cannot see.
6. There are _____ storms in the Bering Sea in winter. In summer there are not as many.
7. Most American universities have a foreign student _____. All students are welcome.
8. _____ Burke rode horseback. At other times he walked.
9. People need _____ to cook and to heat their homes.
10. Children in Canada like to ride downhill on their _____.

B. Vocabulary

tent	terrible	serious	exhausted
broke down	fuel	injured	diary

1. We got home very late because our car _____.
2. Tom _____ himself at work and had to go to the hospital.
3. Some students are very _____ about learning English.
4. Some people like to write in a _____ every day about the things they do and think.
5. Last summer our family went camping in the mountains. We slept in a _____.
6. Ali stayed up all night to study for a test. He was _____ in the morning.
7. There was a _____ fire in an old apartment building, and 10 people died.

C. Vocabulary Review: Antonyms
Match the words with their opposites.

1. huge _____
2. experienced _____
3. get along _____
4. forbid _____
5. complete _____
6. include _____
7. ahead _____
8. separated _____
9. interior _____
10. lack _____
11. ancient _____

a. in back of
b. swamp
c. modern
d. fight
e. together
f. incomplete
g. leave out
h. inexperienced
i. escape
j. allow
k. small
l. exterior
m. have

D. Multiple Choice

1. The first person to reach the South Pole was _____.
   a. English   b. French   c. Norwegian

2. Scott was mainly interested in _____.
   a. being the first person at the South Pole
   b. collecting information about the rocks in Antarctica
   c. learning about the weather and climate in Antarctica

*3. Amundsen's expedition ate dogs because _____.
   a. this is a custom in Norway
   b. it was a way for the men to have fresh meat
   c. there was no other food

*4. Scott's expedition had to travel _____.
   a. a shorter distance than Amundsen's
   b. the same distance as Amundsen's
   c. farther than Amundsen's

*5. January is a _____ month in Antarctica.
   a. summer
   b. fall
   c. winter

6. Scott's trip to the Pole was difficult. The trip back was _____.
   a. more difficult
   b. about the same
   c. much easier

*7. Scott and his men became exhausted because _____.
   a. they didn't have enough fuel, and they could never get warm
   b. the sun on the snow blinded them
   c. they didn't have enough food and had to pull the heavy sleds

8. We know the details about Scott's expedition because _____.
   a. he sent reports back to the English government
   b. he kept a diary, and the search party found it
   c. he wrote detailed letters back to England

E. Comprehension Questions

*1. Scott and Burke led expeditions in very different climates. What was similar about their expeditions?
 2. Explain one serious mistake that Scott made.
*3. Why did Scott travel from his base camp to the Pole in January?
 4. Why did one man walk out of the tent into the blizzard and not return?
 5. Why was it difficult for the men to pull the sleds on the trip back from the Pole?
 6. Why couldn't the three men travel the last 20 kilometers to One Ton Depot?
*7. Was Scott a hero of exploration? Give a reason for your answer.

F. Main Idea

What is the main idea of paragraph 7 (lines 46–55)?

1. moving supplies inland
2. getting ready to ski to the South Pole
3. bad luck with motorized sleds

WORD STUDY

A. Word Forms: Nouns

There are three places in a sentence that always have a noun (or a pronoun): the subject, the object of a verb, and the object of a preposition.

subject	verb	object of the verb	object of a preposition
Neel	rode	a **horse**	to **Tibet**.
The expedition	took	**food**	for the **animals**.
A **storm**	drove	the **ship**	onto an **island**.

The subject is usually at the beginning of a sentence. The object of the verb is usually right after the verb. It answers the question, "What?" The object of a preposition comes after the preposition.

There might be adjectives and other words to describe these nouns.

Neel rode a large black **horse** to **Tibet**.
The large scientific **expedition** took a lot of **food** for their **animals**.
A bad **storm** drove the large sailing **ship** onto a small **island**.

Write the correct word form in the blanks. Use a word from line one in sentence one, and so on. Use the right verb forms and singular or plural nouns.

	Verb	Noun	Adjective	Adverb
1.	include	inclusion	inclusive	inclusively
2.	separate	separation	separate	separately
3.	bury	burial	burial	
4.	realize	realization		
5.	remind	reminder		
6.	inform	information	(un)informative	(un)informatively
7.	organize	organization	organizational	organizationally
8.	injure	injury	injurious	injuriously

1. Did you _____ a description of your dormitory when you wrote to your family?

2a. Amadou's _____ from his family is difficult for him, but he wants to study at a foreign university.

2b. Write your two compositions on _____ pieces of paper. Do them _____.

3. Mr. Byrd died yesterday and they are going to _____ him tomorrow. His _____ is tomorrow.
4. After Ms. Cook got home, she _____ she had forgotten to mail her letters.
5. Ms. Barber put a _____ on the refrigerator for her children to do their homework.
6. Kumiko asked the teacher for _____ about the city buses. The teacher gave her a schedule that was very _____.
7a. An _____ in Melbourne chose Burke to lead an expedition across Australia.
7b. The first meeting of the new club will be an _____ meeting.
8. Chris was in an accident, but luckily he didn't receive any _____.

B. Two-Word Verbs

run out of — use up, not have any more
work out — exercise
slow down — go more slowly
speed up — go faster
live on   — have enough money for necessities

1. Cars have to _____ when they enter a city. When they leave the city, they can _____ again.
2. A lot of people like to go to a gymnasium and _____. This exercise is good for them.
3. The Lopez family adopted two children. Now they can't _____ the money Mr. Lopez earns.
4. Scott's men were hungry because they had almost _____ food.

C. Finding the Reason

Here are some sentences about the explorers you have read about. Give a reason for each statement. The first one is done for you.

Statement	Reason
1. Scott and his men were cold all the time.	They didn't have enough fuel.
2. Scott went to the South Pole.	
3. Neel studied Tibetan in India.	
4. Bering's expedition lost a lot of their food.	
5. Bering took scientists with him.	
6. Burke died on his expedition.	
7. Burke took camels on his expedition.	
8. The world knows about Burke's and Scott's expeditions.	

D. Context Clues

1. When Scott returned from his first expedition to Antarctica, he gave **lectures** to organizations. People wanted to hear about his journey.
   a. movies that he took in Antarctica
   b. speeches that give information
   c. long articles full of information from his diaries

2. Mr. Mora told his son, "Stop fighting with your sister. If you don't **behave**, you'll have to go to bed right now."
   a. stay awake   b. act correctly   c. slow down

3. A **wool** sweater is much warmer than a cotton or polyester one.
   a. cloth made from animal skin
   b. cloth from a plant
   c. cloth from sheep's hair

4. It is **amazing** that a woman was able to travel all over the interior of China and Tibet by herself.
   a. very surprising   b. terrible   c. frequent

5. Maria has a very bad **attitude** toward learning English. She thinks that if she just listens in class, she can learn everything she needs. Outside of class, she just wants to have fun.
   a. equipment
   b. way of thinking
   c. good experience

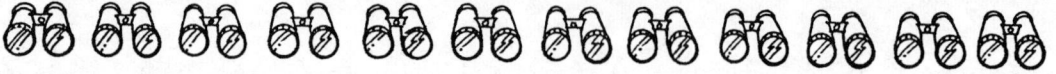

MARY KINGSLEY— VICTORIAN EXPLORER

5

Mary Kingsley spent 18 months exploring West Africa between 1893 and 1895. The two books she wrote and the **lectures** she gave back in England about her travels helped to change
5 the way Europeans thought about their African colonies. Kingsley also helped to start anthropology, the study of people's customs and lives, in Africa. We must understand something about English life at that time in order to understand
10 how **amazing** this was.

Mary Kingsley was born near London in 1862 and grew up while Victoria was queen of England. At that time women were expected to stay at home, take care of their husbands and
15 children, and behave like ladies.

Mary's father was a doctor and her mother was his cook. The parents got married only four days before Mary was born. Her father spent most of his time traveling in far off countries,
20 and he hardly ever came home. Her mother was never well and spent her life in her bedroom with all the curtains closed. Of course Mary had to take care of her, so Mary never married. She never went to school either; she had to educate
25 herself.

When both her parents died in 1892, Mary took the money they left her and went to visit the Canary Islands off the coast of West Africa.

educational speeches

very surprising

She met traders there, European men who
30 bought rubber, ivory, which comes from elephants, and other products from Africans and
sold them things from Europe. She returned to
England and studied to do useful scientific work
in West Africa. During her first trip of 6 months
35 back to West Africa and her second one of nearly
a year, she collected fish for the British Museum.
Much more important, she gathered information about African customs, law, and religion.
European men had been exploring Africa
40 for years. Each explorer took large amounts of
equipment, food, and other supplies and needed
many Africans to carry them. The Europeans
had guns and used them when there was trouble. Kingsley traveled with only six Africans to
45 help her. She slept in village houses and ate what
the Africans ate. She had a gun, but she never
shot anyone. She always wore a white cotton
blouse and a long wool skirt. She was usually the
first white woman the villagers had ever seen,
50 but they accepted her as a friend because of the
way she traveled. She was able to ask them all
kinds of questions about their lives and later
wrote detailed scientific descriptions of African
customs. She also wrote beautiful descriptions of
55 the slow-moving rivers, the sounds of the African night, and the beauty of the African forest.
At that time there were three groups of
Europeans in Africa. They were the traders, the
people working for the colonial governments,
60 and missionaries who went to Africa to teach
Christianity. They all believed that Europeans
were **superior to** other people. They believed   better than
either that Africans were wild or that they were
childlike. The English missionaries believed Af-
65 ricans and Europeans were brothers because
they were all God's children, but they also believed that Africans were inferior because they
were not Christians. The missionaries thought

that the Africans' false religion made them live
70 inferior lives, but if they started wearing European clothes, learned English, forgot their old
ways, and became Christians, they could become
better people. The other Europeans believed
that Africans were inferior and less intelligent
75 than white people.

As Mary Kingsley gathered information
about African customs, she learned that their
religion was the center of their lives. Their religion and customs, even the ones that seemed
80 very strange to Europeans, all fit together in a
logical way. She believed that if Europeans tried
to change African religion or any of their other
customs, the Africans' lives would be worse than
before. However, she also believed that Africans
85 could not learn technology and could never move
into the modern world. As she wrote and lec-
tured about her ideas, the men working in the
colonial governments learned from her, and the
governments became better.

90 When Kingsley reached a village, she usually said, "It's only me." She said it so often that
villagers started calling her "Only Me" because
they thought it was her name. She was European, so the Africans treated her like a European
95 and not like a woman. She had much more
freedom than she had when she was at home in
England.

In 1900, Kingsley went to South Africa to
help in the hospitals during the Boer War, but
100 she planned to return to West Africa. However,
in a short time she became sick and died at the
age of 37. She was buried at sea.

Mary Kingsley was a Victorian woman. She
became an explorer, geographer, anthropologist,
105 and author. Today it is not easy for a woman to
be even one of these things. In Kingsley's time it
was almost impossible, but she was all of them.
Her books started a change in West African

history because they helped change the **atti-**
110 **tudes** of the Europeans toward the Africans in
their colonies. Her great knowledge of African
customs helped start the anthropological study
of Africa. She was an amazing woman.

A. Vocabulary

products	educated	anthropology	colony
lecture	ivory	missionary	behave
childlike	superior	treats	inferior

1. Mona is the best student in the class. She is _____ to all
   the other students. They are _____ to her.
2. Pierre is Canadian, but he didn't go to school in Canada. He was _____
   _____ in France.
3. Professor Allen will give a _____ today about his research
   on fish that live in caves.
4. A _____ tries to get people to change their religion.
5. Some people are born with inferior intelligence. They are _____
   all their lives. They never act like grownups.
6. Japan produces cars, televisions, computers, and other _____.
7. Carlos always _____ older people politely.
8. Hong Kong is a British _____.
9. Susan is going to study _____ .

B. Vocabulary

behave	trade	accept	rubber
wool	ivory	attitude	technology
amazing	product	anthropology	logical

1. The twentieth century is the age of _____. We have computers and other amazing machines.
2. Farmers raise sheep for their meat and _____ in New
   Zealand, Europe, and other areas of the world.

3. When we study the history of the world, the importance of _____ between countries is clear.
4. People make beautiful things from _____ which comes from elephants.
5. Isamu says the reading book is too easy for him, so he never studies. Yet he always gets bad grades. This is not _____ thinking. If he changes his _____, he can get good grades.
6. Sometimes children _____ badly in school.
7. _____ comes from trees and is used to make tires for cars and trucks.
8. It is _____ that today people in some remote areas know nothing about the rest of the world.
9. When you live in another country, you have to _____ the people and the customs there. You cannot change them.

C. Vocabulary Review

beggar	surrounded	temperature	civil war
delayed	in order to	sink	ashore
decade	organization	tent	terrible

1. The soldiers _____ the building so no one could escape.
2. Every year ships _____ in storms.
3. The snowstorm _____ us 3 hours because we had to drive very slowly.
4. A _____ asks people for money or food.
5. OPEC means the _____ of Petroleum Exporting Countries.
6. Did you ever sleep outdoors in a _____?
7. There has been a _____ in Lebanon for several years. Different groups of Lebanese are fighting among themselves.
8. Sometimes the summer _____ in Antarctica is −40°C.
9. A _____ forest fire burned thousands of hectares of trees.
10. A _____ is 10 years.

D. True/False

_____ 1. Mary Kingsley spent a total of 2 years exploring in West Africa.
_____ 2. Mary had to educate herself.
_____ 3. Traders buy and sell things.
_____ *4. European explorers sometimes shot Africans.
_____ *5. A long wool skirt and white blouse are good clothes for exploring in West Africa.
_____ 6. Kingsley took a lot of equipment with her because she was doing scientific research on fish.
_____ *7. English missionaries believed that all people are God's children.
_____ 8. The West African religion was the center of all their customs.
_____ *9. Kingsley believed that Africans could not learn technology.
_____ 10. Kingsley became sick and died in West Africa.

E. Comprehension Questions

1. What was a woman's life like in Victorian England?
2. How did Mary Kingsley tell others about her research in Africa?
3. Why didn't she go to school?
4. Where did she get the money to go to the Canary Islands?
5. What are traders?
6. What are missionaries?
7. What is a colony?
8. How were Kingsley's expeditions different from the expeditions of European men?
9. How did Kingsley do her research?
10. What did Kingsley believe about trying to change African customs?
11. How did her books help change West African history?

F. Main Idea
What is the main idea of paragraph 9 (lines 98–102)?

1. Kingsley worked in a hospital in South Africa.
2. Kingsley died in South Africa in 1900.
3. Kingsley was buried at sea.

WORD STUDY

A. Articles: The
Some geographical locations include **the** in the name.

1. Certain countries (Note: Most countries do *not* include **the** in the name.)
   the United States of America or the United States or the U.S.A. or the U.S.
   the Union of Soviet Socialist Republics or the Soviet Union or the USSR
   the United Arab Emirates
   the United Kingdom
   the Philippines
   the Netherlands

2. Major points on the earth:
   the North Pole
   the South Pole
   the Equator

3. Plurals of islands, lakes, and mountains:
   the Canary Islands
   the Great Lakes
   the Himalaya Mountains

4. Oceans, seas, rivers, canals, deserts:
   the Pacific Ocean
   the Bering Sea
   the Mississippi River
   the Suez Canal
   the Sahara Desert

5. Continents, most geographical areas, most countries, and single islands, lakes, and mountains do not have **the** in the name.
   Asia
   Western Europe but **the Middle East**
   England
   Bering Island
   Lake Geneva
   Mount Everest

EXPLORERS

Write **the** in the blanks if it is necessary.

1. _____ Panama Canal joins _____ Atlantic Ocean and _____ Pacific Ocean.
2. This canal used to belong to _____ United States.
3. _____ Kuwait is near _____ United Arab Emirates and _____ Saudi Arabia.
4. _____ Germany, _____ Belgium, and _____ Netherlands are in _____ Europe.
5. _____ Lake Geneva is in _____ Switzerland.
6. Where are _____ Madeira Islands?
7. _____ Poland is near _____ USSR.
8. _____ Jordan is in _____ Middle East.
9. _____ Amazon River is in _____ South America.

B. Word Forms: Nouns

These are some common noun suffixes:

-er, **-ar**, **-or**: reminder, beggar, advisor
-ist: scientist
-ment: equipment
-ion, **-sion**, **-tion**, **-ation**: religion, decision, separation, realization
-y: discovery
-ity: electricity
-ness: happiness
-ance: acceptance

Put the right form of the word in each sentence.

	Verb	Noun	Adjective	Adverb
1.	trade	trade		
		trader		
2.	produce	product	(un)productive	(un)productively
		production		
3.	accept	acceptance	(un)acceptable	(un)acceptably
4.	(mis)behave	(mis)behavior		
5.	educate	education	(un)educated	
6.	treat	treatment		
7.	amaze	amazement	amazing	amazingly
8.	colonize	colony	colonial	
		colonist		

1. Japan and Saudi Arabia _____ with each other.
2a. Mexico's _____ of oil is higher this year than last.
2b. It is _____ to translate each lesson into your language. This is not a good way to study English.
3. Your homework is not _____ because the teacher can't read it.
4. The children are on their good _____ because they are going to a party.
5. _____ is very important for everyone.
6. The boss _____ Ann very badly during the meeting.
7. Ali looked with _____ at the tall buildings in New York. They are _____ high.
8. France _____ North Africa in the nineteenth century.

C. Prepositions

Write the correct preposition in the blanks.

1. Anthropology is the study _____ people's customs and lives.
2. We must understand something _____ English life _____ that time _____ order to understand how amazing this was.
3. _____ that time women were expected to stay _____ home, take care _____ their husbands and children, and behave like ladies.
4. Her mother spent her life _____ her bedroom _____ all the curtains closed.
5. Mary took the money they left her and went to visit the Canary Islands _____ the coast _____ West Africa.
6. She studied to do useful scientific work _____ West Africa.
7. _____ her first trip _____ 6 months and her second one _____ 18 months, she collected fish _____ the British Museum.
8. They accepted her as a friend because _____ the way she traveled.
9. They all believed that Europeans were superior _____ other people.

D. Scanning

When you want to find just one detail in a text, it is not necessary to read carefully. You **scan** instead; that is, you look as quickly as possible until you find the information.

EXPLORERS

Find these answers by scanning. Write short answers (not complete sentences). Write the number of the line where you found each answer.

1. When was Mary Kingsley born?
2. What did she wear on her expeditions?
3. What did Africans call her?
4. How old was she when she died?
5. When did her parents die?
6. Why did missionaries go to Africa?
7. Who was queen when Kingsley was born?
8. What was the name of the war in South Africa in 1900?
9. Kingsley was an explorer. What else was she?

E. Context Clues

1. What is the answer when you add these **figures**: 739, 526, and 43?
   a. numbers   b. kilometers   c. kilos

2. Petroleum, iron, rich farmland, and coal for making electricity are all **natural resources**.
   a. anything people can use
   b. anything people make
   c. anything from nature that people can use

3. What is the best **method** to learn a language?
   a. lesson   b. way   c. composition

4. When two crowded trains run into each other, this is a **disaster**. When heavy rains cause a river to flood a village, this is also a **disaster**.
   a. anything terrible caused by people
   b. anything terrible caused by nature
   c. anything terrible that happens

5. A **shortage** of food in a poor country can cause people to die of hunger.
   a. poor farmland
   b. not enough
   c. plants that are not tall enough

6. A few tickets for the basketball game are still **available**, but you should buy one as soon as possible before they are all sold out.
   a. You can get one.
   b. They didn't make any.
   c. These tickets are too expensive.

7. When we meet a group of people from another country, it is easy to think that they are all alike; they look similar and think in the same way. But this is not true. Each one is really an **individual**.
   a. part of a group
   b. a different, separate person
   c. similar to the other people in the family

Unit II

WORLD ISSUES

Our responsibility is to protect the Earth for a million years.
—Robert Hunter
one of the organizers of Greenpeace

WORLD POPULATION GROWTH

Is the world overpopulated? How many people can the earth support? Should countries try to limit their **population**? These are serious questions that governments, international orga-
5 nizations, and **individuals** must think about.

The population of the world has been increasing faster and faster. In 10,000 B.C. there were probably only 10 million people. In A.D. 1 there were 300 million. It took 1750 years for the
10 population to reach 625 million, a little more than double the A.D. 1 **figure.** In 1850, only 100 years later, the population had nearly doubled again, with a figure of 1130 million. In 1950, the figure had more than doubled to reach 2510
15 million. In 1985, only 35 years later, there were 4760 million people. By 2000, the world's population is expected to be over 6 billion.

Seventy-five percent of the world's population live in Third World countries. This means
20 that most people are poor and are unable to give children a good life.

Does the earth have enough natural resources to support this many people? Different scientists give different answers to this question.
25 Some say that there are enough resources to support more than 6 billion people, but the problem is distribution. The richest countries, with a small percentage of the world's population, use

number of people in an area

individual = one person

number

51

most of the resources. If these resources could be
30 distributed equally, there would be enough for
everyone.

    Other scientists say that we must limit pop-
ulation growth because our resources are limited. Only 10 percent of the earth's land can be
35 used for farming and another 20 percent for
raising animals. It is possible to increase the
amount of farmland, but only a little. Some land
in developing countries can be more productive
if people start using modern farming **methods**,   ways
40 but this will not increase worldwide production
very much.

    We all know that there is a limited amount
of petroleum. There are also limits to the
amounts of iron (Fe), silver (Ag), gold (Au), and
45 other metals. There is a limit to the water we can
use — most of the earth's water is salt water, and
most of the fresh water is frozen at the North
and South Poles.

    Even some of the world's "natural" **disas-**
50 **ters** are partly caused by overpopulation. We all   terrible things that happen
know about the terrible famine, with thousands
of people dying of hunger, in Ethiopia in the
1980s. The famine area of Ethiopia used to be
forested. Forests hold water in the ground, but
55 in Ethiopia too many people cut down too many
trees for firewood. In only 20 years, the forests
were gone. At the same time there were several
years without rain and farmland became desert.
There was no food and people died of hunger.

60   It is difficult to say how many people the
earth can support, but it will help everyone if we
can limit population growth before serious
shortages develop. The problem is how to do it.

    Each individual must decide to help limit
65 population. Each person must decide how many
children to have. But there are many reasons
that people want to have several children. Some
people, because of their religion, believe that

they must accept every child that God sends
70 them. In countries where many children die before they can grow up, people think they need to
have several children. Then the parents will
have someone to take care of them when they
are old. In some countries it is very important to
75 men that they have sons instead of daughters.
They want to keep having children until they
have several sons.

Research has repeatedly shown that the
average Third World woman has more children
80 than she wants. Among the women who do not
think they have too many children, half of them
do not want any more; they think they already
have enough. However, although millions of
women in the world want to limit the size of
85 their families, they know of no safe way to have
fewer children. Safe birth-control methods for
family planning are not available to them.

Governments and international organiza-
tions can **provide** safe, inexpensive birth-   give
90 control methods. Individuals can decide to use
them. Then the world population growth can
decrease instead of continuing to increase.

A. Vocabulary

limit	figures	method	shortage
control	increases	raise	disaster
although	provide	overpopulated	resources

1. _____ most journalists studied journalism in college, some
   older writers never attended a university.
2. Can you explain the _____ for changing salt water to fresh
   water?
3. The number of injuries from automobile accidents _____
   every year.
4. Some countries are poor because they have very few natural _____.

5. The Red Cross helps when there is a _____.
6. These are all _____: 1, 75, 293.
7. Some governments _____ scholarships so people can attend university.
8. A lack of rain can cause a water _____.
9. China has a billion people. Is it _____?
10. There is a _____ of 20 minutes for this short test. Students must turn in their papers at the end of 20 minutes.

B. Vocabulary

control	international	metals	average
decreasing	individual	distribution	famine
limit	raised	available	population

1. What is the _____ of your country? Is it increasing?
2. _____ are one kind of natural resource.
3. The population of Ireland is _____. There are fewer people now than 10 years ago.
4. The _____ of 8, 5, 9, 3, and 6 is 6.2.
5. Some children behave badly and their parents can't _____ them.
6. Coffee is _____ in Central and South America.
7. When there is a _____ in a country, other countries send food for _____ to the hungry people.
8. Every person in the class is a different kind of _____.
9. People build houses of the materials that are _____ in the area.
10. The United Nations is an _____ organization.

C. Vocabulary Review

skill	tent	each other	blind
diary	frequently	surrounded	adventure
exhausted	civil war	yet	ashore

1. Mr. Rossi was _____ after driving for 10 hours.
2. Our children had a wonderful _____. They went camping in Canada, slept in a _____, and helped cook their food outdoors over an open fire.

3. Typing is a very useful _____ for students. They can learn by practicing.
4. The world is overpopulated, _____ people keep having large families.
5. Alice injured her eyes in an accident. Now she is _____.
6. There was a terrible _____ in Spain in the 1930s. Almost a million people died.
7. Some composition teachers have the students keep a _____. They write about their activities and their thoughts.
8. Mexican and African students have to speak English to _____.
9. The children _____ the man who was giving away free candy.
10. Glen _____ goes to the movies on weekends.

WORLD POPULATION

Date	Population
10,000 B.C.	10,000,000
1 A.D.	300,000,000
1750 A.D.	625,000,000
1850 A.D.	1,130,000,000
1950 A.D.	2,510,000,000
1985 A.D.	4,760,000,000
2000 A.D.	6,600,000,000

WORLD POPULATION BY REGION

Region	Percent
South Asia	32%
East Asia	26%
Europe	11%
Africa	10%
Latin America	8%
USSR	6%
Northern America	6%
Oceania	1%

THE WORLD'S LARGEST COUNTRIES IN POPULATION

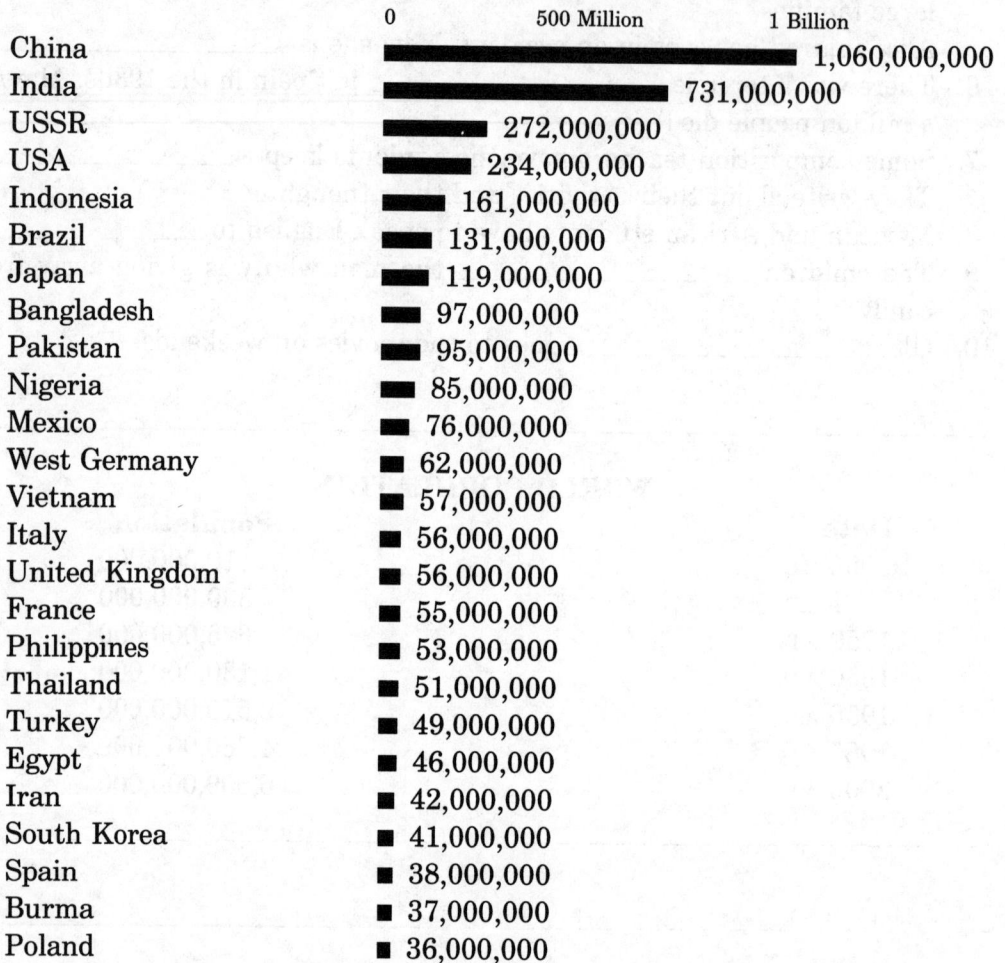

Country		Population
	0 500 Million 1 Billion	
China		1,060,000,000
India		731,000,000
USSR		272,000,000
USA		234,000,000
Indonesia		161,000,000
Brazil		131,000,000
Japan		119,000,000
Bangladesh		97,000,000
Pakistan		95,000,000
Nigeria		85,000,000
Mexico		76,000,000
West Germany		62,000,000
Vietnam		57,000,000
Italy		56,000,000
United Kingdom		56,000,000
France		55,000,000
Philippines		53,000,000
Thailand		51,000,000
Turkey		49,000,000
Egypt		46,000,000
Iran		42,000,000
South Korea		41,000,000
Spain		38,000,000
Burma		37,000,000
Poland		36,000,000

D. Multiple Choice

For the rest of the book, there are no asterisks (*) before any questions. You have to decide if the answer is in one of the sentences, or if you have to figure it out for yourself. In this exercise, use the text, the chart, and the graphs to answer the questions.

1. There were almost _____ as many people in the world in 1985 as in 1950.
   a. twice   b. three times   c. four times

2. Between 1985 and 2000, the world population will _____.
   a. more than double
   b. be more than three times as large
   c. increase by nearly two billion

3. About _____ percent of the earth's land can be used for raising food.
   a. 10   b. 20   c. 30

4. A _____ is sometimes a natural disaster.
   a. plane accident   b. forest fire   c. ship sinking

5. In the Third World, _____ women want more children.
   a. most   b. some   c. no

6. Safe birth-control methods are _____.
   a. usually expensive
   b. not available for some women
   c. never used by religious people

7. _____ are the same size.
   a. The USSR and the U.S.
   b. Britain and Italy
   c. Burma and Poland

8. _____ is the region with the largest population.
   a. Africa   b. South Asia   c. The USSR

9. In _____ the population of the whole world was about the same as the population of China today.
   a. 1750   b. 1850   c. 1950

10. The country of _____ has the same population as Canada and the U.S.
    a. India   b. Russia   c. Indonesia

E. Comprehension Questions

Use the text, charts, and graphs to answer these questions.

1. Do more people live in developed or developing countries?
2. Explain the problem of distribution of natural resources.

3. Can the amount of farmland be increased?
4. Why can't we use most of the earth's water?
5. Which European countries are among the world's largest?
6. How many people can the earth support?
7. Give two reasons that people have big families.
8. Do most Third World women want a lot of children?
9. What was one of the causes of the famine in Ethiopia?
10. What region of the world has the smallest population?
11. Do you think your country has too many people? Give a reason for your answer.

F. Main Idea
What is the main idea of paragraph 2 (lines 6–17)? Write it in a sentence.

WORD STUDY

A. Word Forms: Adjectives

Adjectives describe nouns. They are usually before the noun. Sometimes they are alone after the verb **be**.

> These are **serious** questions.
> These questions are **serious**.

The participle form of a verb, past or present, is often used as an adjective. The past participle is the third form of the verb; for example, talk, talked, **talked** and freeze, froze, **frozen**. The present participle is the -**ing** form of the verb; for example, **talking**.

> The world is **overpopulated**.
> **Increasing** population is a problem.

Write the correct word forms in the blanks.

	Verb	Noun	Adjective	Adverb
1.		history	historical	historically
2.		shortage	short	
3.		disaster	disastrous	
4.	distribute	distribution		
5.	populate	population		
6.	care	care	careful/careless	carefully/carelessly
7.	use	use	useful/useless	usefully/uselessly
8.		individual	individual	individually
9.		nation	national	nationally

1. Anne likes to read _____ novels.
2a. The secretary was _____ of paper and had to order some. She didn't have enough.
2b. There was a _____ of coffee because thousands of coffee trees in Brazil froze.
3. A famine is _____ for a country.
4. The professor always _____ the test papers as soon as the bell rings.
5. What is the _____ of your country?

6. If you are _____ when you write your composition, you will probably get a good grade. If you write _____, you may fail.
7. A sled is _____ if you live in Kuwait.
8. The kind of car a person buys is an _____ decision. Each person must decide _____.
9. Baseball is the _____ sport in the United States.

B. Two-Word Verbs

cut down — cut down a tree, for example
figure out — find the answer
make up — think of a new story or idea
hang up — end a telephone conversation
clear up — clouds disappear and the sun comes out

1. It was rainy and cloudy this morning, but now it is starting to _____.
2. The big old tree in our front yard is dead. We have to _____ it _____.
3. I can't _____ the answer to this math problem.
4. When Tom finished talking to his friend on the phone, he said "Good-bye" and then _____.
5. Mr. Hasegawa _____ funny stories to tell his children.

C. Irregular Verbs
Memorize these verb forms. Then put the right form of a verb in the blanks.

Simple	Past	Past Participle
freeze	froze	frozen
forbid	forbade	forbidden
sink	sank	sunk
shoot	shot	shot

1. The law _____ driving over 40 kilometers an hour on side streets in the city. You can drive 60 or 75 on main streets.
2. A small sailboat hit a rock and _____.
3. _____ food is quick and easy to cook.
4. Bob went hunting and _____ a bear.

D. Articles
Put an article in the blank if one is necessary.

1. Is _____ world overpopulated?
2. How many people can _____ earth support?
3. These are _____ serious questions that _____ people must think about.
4. _____ different scientists give _____ different answers to these questions.
5. One of _____ problems is _____ distribution.
6. _____ richest countries, with _____ small percentage of _____ world's population, use _____ most of _____ resources.
7. It is possible to increase _____ amount of _____ farmland, but only _____ little.
8. We all know that there is _____ limited amount of _____ petroleum.
9. We all know about _____ terrible famine, with _____ thousands of people dying of _____ hunger, in _____ Ethiopia in _____ 1980s.

E. Context Clues

1. Saudi Arabian **society** is very different from Japan's. People dress differently in the two countries. Religion is very important in Saudi Arabia but it isn't in Japan. Holidays are different. Homes are different. Most Japanese live in large cities. Most Saudis do not. The languages are different. The life of women is different.
   a. the way people spend their time
   b. everything about the life in a country
   c. the life of each individual woman

2. The aborigines have been in Australia for 10,000 years. Their **ancestors** probably came from South Asia.
   a. people in the family a long time ago
   b. people in the family in the future
   c. great-grandparents

3. Elaine is an electrician. She **earns** 12 dollars an hour.
   a. works
   b. is paid for working
   c. pays

4. Al has a difficult problem to **solve** for his engineering class.
   a. write   b. read   c. figure out

CHANGES IN THE FAMILY

2

Sociologists study society and how it is organized. They study what a society believes and how it is changing. They explain how people behave, but not how they ought to behave.

5   Almost every society is based on the family. Some societies have a nuclear family. In the nuclear family the parents and children live together in one house. Other societies have an extended family. In this kind of family there are
10 grandparents, parents, children, uncles, and other relatives all living together. In some societies there are tribes. A tribe is a group of extended families who have the same ancestors. In North and South America, the members of an
15 Indian tribe speak the same language. Each tribe in Africa has its own language too. In Saudi Arabia and the other Gulf countries, the tribes all speak Arabic.

    Sometimes the power of the extended family or the tribe is based on the land that they
20 own.

    Everybody in a family knows how to behave as a family member. Children learn how to act like grownups by watching the adults in their
25 family. They learn how a father or mother should behave. Everyone knows what the correct behavior is, and relatives like to talk about this. "Is Kumiko acting the way a mother should

act?" "Does Abdullah behave in the right way
30 for a husband?"

It is hard to look at research about the
family with our minds instead of our feelings.
Each person is part of a family and a society and
knows what a family should be like. It is hard to
35 realize that one kind of family can fit a society
very well, even if it is very different from the
family in our society.

Throughout history there have been slow
changes in the family and family life, but today
40 the family is changing quickly. This change
causes many problems for the society and the
individual.

One of the major reasons for this fast
change in the family is the change in how people
45 earn their money. Today more and more people
work in factories that make automobiles, furniture, clothes, and thousands of other products.
Fewer people work on farms or make products at
home. People work in industry instead. This
50 change is called industrialization. The ownership of land in an industrial society is not as
important as it was when people lived in villages.

For decades young people have been leaving
farms and small towns to go to cities and work in
55 factories. They often find a wife or husband in
the city instead of marrying someone from their
village. They start their own family away from
their old home. These young people often have
more money than the old people in their family.
60 In village life, young people went to the old
people with their questions and problems. The
old people had lived a long time and had more
knowledge. However, as young people moved to
cities, got more education, and learned technol-
65 ogy, they discovered that the old people in their
family did not have all the answers to their
questions about life. Their new lives in the city
were too different from village life. Also, in some

countries, the government started to make laws
70 about things the tribe used to decide.

Life continued to change, and the children
of these young people discovered that their city
parents didn't always have the answers either.
Life was changing too fast.

75 Since the end of World War II, industrialization has been increasing very fast throughout
the world. This is causing family life to change
faster too. Societies are losing their extended
families. More married couples want their own
80 home where they can live with their children.

The West has had nuclear families instead
of extended families at least since the Industrial
Revolution. The Industrial Revolution started in
England around 1760, when people changed
85 from making things by hand to making them in
factories.

Western families are changing too. When
people get a good education and good jobs, they
can improve their lives. They realize that if they
90 have fewer children, they can give them a better
life. Now more women work outside the home,
and they delay having children. The size of families gets smaller. In the United States, some of
these small nuclear families move several times,
95 each time earning more money and improving
their lives. Some young couples don't see their
parents very often. They don't think it is necessary to invite their parents to live with them
when they are old. Many of the old parents don't
100 want to live with their grown children either.

As Third World countries industrialize,
they find they are having the same problems
that Western families have. If a country modernizes and industrializes fast, the family
105 changes fast. Many old people want life to continue as it was. Young people want to move
ahead and change. These different ideas can
cause problems in the family.

110 We can learn about these changes in the family from sociologists and understand why problems are developing. It is helpful for us to understand what is happening to our societies, but each individual family must try to solve its problems for itself.

A. Vocabulary

individual	solve	earn	revolution
throughout	ancestors	industrial	industry
tribes	extended	nuclear	sociologists

1. The _____ family is larger than the _____ family.
2. There have been some civil wars between different African _____ living in the same country.
3. The _____ of everyone in Canada came from other countries. The Indians were the first to arrive.
4. How much money does a secretary _____?
5. If every _____ in the world told the government he or she wouldn't fight, we wouldn't have any more wars.
6. Japan is an _____ nation. It has both heavy and light _____.

B. Vocabulary

extend	industrial	earn	solve
member	factory	sociologist	throughout
revolution	societies	tribe	relatives

1. Maria is from Mexico, but she has several _____ in California. Three of her aunts live there with their families.
2. Sam works in an airplane _____.
3. Karl is a _____ of the International Students Organization.
4. A _____ does research about _____ throughout the world.

5. Governments _____ the world are trying to _____ the problems in their country.

6. The Russian _____ was in 1917. There was a complete change in government.

C. Vocabulary Review

Match each word with its definition.

1. blizzard _____
2. inland _____
3. wool _____
4. pony _____
5. overeat _____
6. inferior _____
7. trade _____
8. break down _____
9. superior _____
10. work out _____

a. small horse
b. buying and selling
c. worse than
d. stop running or working
e. a kind of cloth
f. a bad snow and wind storm
g. missionaries
h. exercise
i. anthropology
j. away from the ocean
k. eat more than you should
l. better than

D. True/False

_____ 1. Sociologists tell us how people should behave so they can improve their society.

_____ 2. Members of a tribe all have the same ancestors.

_____ 3. Each individual learns how to fit in the family and society by copying the people around her or him.

_____ 4. The family is changing fast because of industrialization.

_____ 5. In many countries, the life of young people is very different from the life of their grandparents.

_____ 6. The West had extended families until the twentieth century.

_____ 7. When a country modernizes fast, the family changes fast.

_____ 8. The Industrial Revolution was a civil war in England. People fought about the ownership of land.

_____ 9. As countries industrialize, the family size decreases.

E. Comprehension Questions

1. What is a nuclear family?
2. What is a tribe?
3. Why can't the old people in a family always help young people solve their problems?
4. When did industrialization start increasing throughout the world?
5. Why do many American families move several times?
6. Is your country already industrialized, or is it now developing industries?
7. In your country, is the family life of your friends different from the family life of your grandparents when they were young? Give two examples.

F. Main Idea

What is the main idea of paragraph 2 (lines 5–18)? Write it in a sentence.

WORD STUDY

A. Word Forms: Adjectives

These are some common adjective suffixes: **-able**, **-al**, **-ful**, **-ive**, **-less**, **-like**, **-ous**, **-t**, **-y**.

Put the right word forms in the blanks.

	Verb	Noun	Adjective	Adverb
1.		society	social	socially
2.	industrialize	industry	industrial	
3.	earn	earnings		
4.		tribe	tribal	
5.	control	control	(un)controllable	(un)controllably
6.	limit	limit	limitless (un)limited	
7.		logic	(il)logical	(il)logically
8.		fame	famous	
9.		distance	distant	
10.	storm	storm	stormy	

1. Industrialization causes serious _____ problems in a country.
2. Many Third World countries are trying hard to _____.
3. Mr. and Mrs. Novak have to spend all of their _____ to support their family.
4. There have been many _____ wars in Africa.
5. A tire blew out and the car was _____. It went out of _____ and hit a tree.
6. Some people think there is a(n) _____ amount of petroleum in the world, but some day we will run out.
7. Pat figured out the problem by using _____.
8. Pele was a _____ soccer player.
9. Alexandra David-Neel visited _____, mysterious areas of the world.
10. _____ weather caused serious problems for Vitus Bering.

B. Prepositions
Put a preposition in the blanks.

1. Almost every society is based _____ the family.
2. _____ some societies there are tribes.
3. _____ North America, the members _____ an Indian tribe speak the same language.
4. Sometimes the power _____ the family or the tribe is based _____ the land that they own.
5. Children learn how to act _____ watching the adults _____ their family.
6. It is hard to look _____ research _____ the family _____ our minds instead _____ our feelings.
7. One _____ the major reasons _____ the fast change _____ the family is industrialization.
8. _____ decades young people have been leaving farms to go _____ cities and work _____ factories.
9. They start their own family _____ _____ their old home.
10. The Industrial Revolution was when people changed _____ making things _____ hand _____ making them _____ factories.

C. Summarizing
A **summary** is a short description of all the important information in a paragraph or text. A summary of a paragraph is usually just one sentence. A summary of a complete reading text has a few sentences.

Choose the summary sentence for these paragraphs.

1. Paragraph 1 (lines 1–4)
   a. Sociologists study how a society is changing.
   b. Sociologists study society.
   c. Sociologists study how people behave.

2. Paragraph 2 (lines 5–18)
   a. Societies have extended and nuclear families and sometimes tribes.
   b. A nuclear family is small, and an extended family is much larger.
   c. Almost every society is based on the family, either nuclear or extended.

3. Paragraph 4 (lines 22–30)
   a. Everyone learns how to behave as a parent.
   b. Everyone learns how to behave from other family members.
   c. Children learn how to behave by watching adult family members.

4. Paragraph 6 (lines 38–42)
   a. The family is changing fast today, and this causes problems.
   b. When families change, it causes problems for the individual.
   c. The family is changing faster today than before.

5. Paragraph 7 (lines 43–52)
   a. One cause of this change is working in factories.
   b. One cause of this change is owning land.
   c. One cause of this change is industrialization.

D. Context Clues

1. Dean grew up on a farm, and he plans to study **agriculture**. Then he wants to buy a farm of his own.
   a. biology   b. farming   c. sociology

2. Dean's family has a small farm. They have two **fields** of wheat, one of corn, and several of vegetables. They use another **field** for their cows and horses.
   a. a garden
   b. the area of a farm where grass or other plants grow
   c. the place where farmers keep their animals

3. Mr. Martin has a good job. He **trains** new workers for McDonald's. They have to learn how to do their jobs before they start work.
   a. teaches   b. travels   c. raises

4. Ann has to **prepare** for her parents' visit to her apartment. She is going to clean and then buy food so she can cook dinner.
   a. telephone   b. invite   c. get ready

5. Amadou **is supposed to** give a report in class today. He didn't prepare, however, so he decided not to go to class.
   a. should   b. might   c. can

WOMEN AND CHANGE

3

Women hold up half the sky. This is an old Chinese saying. However, research shows that perhaps women do more than their share of "holding up the sky."

5   In 1975, the United Nations organized the Decade for Women. In 1985, it published a report on the conditions and rights of women throughout the world.

Some of the news in the report is very good. 10 For example, 90 percent of all countries now have official organizations to improve the lives of women. More than half the countries have laws to protect the rights of women. Ninety percent of the countries have passed laws to give women 15 equal pay for equal work. WHO (World Health Organization) and UNICEF (United Nations Children's Fund) have programs to improve the health of people in Third World countries, especially women and children. Half of the women in 20 the world now have birth-control methods available. Forty-one percent of the children in school now are girls, a big change from the past, because in many countries education was not available to girls.

25   The report also has bad news. Although most countries have official organizations to improve women's lives, many of these organizations don't do anything. Fifty percent of the

world's population are women, but in nearly
30 two-thirds of all working hours the work is done
by women. They do most of the domestic work,
for example, cooking and washing clothes. Millions also work outside the home. Women hold
35 percent of all the world's jobs. For this work,
35 they earn only 40 to 60 percent as much as men,
and of course they earn nothing for their domestic work.

Only 6 percent of places in government are
held by women. Sixty percent of the people who
40 can't read and write are women. It is these
illiterate women who are the most **frightened**   afraid
of trying to improve their lives. Being illiterate
doesn't mean they are not intelligent. It does
mean it is difficult for them to change their lives.
45 In developing countries, where three-
fourths of the world's population lives, women
produce more than half of the food. In Africa, 80
percent of all **agricultural** work is done by   farming
women. There are many programs to help poor
50 countries develop their agriculture. However,
for years these programs **provided** money and   gave
training for men and not for women. Now that   teaching
the UN report is published, this is changing.
International organizations and programs run
55 by developed nations are starting to help women,
as well as men, improve their agricultural production.

In parts of Africa, this is a **typical** day for   usual
a village woman. At 4:45 a.m. she gets up,
60 washes, and eats. It takes her a half hour to walk
to the fields, and she works there until 3:00 p.m.
She collects firewood and gets home at 4:00. She
spends the next hour and a half **preparing** food   getting ready
to cook. Then she collects water for another
65 hour. From 6:30 to 8:30 she cooks. After dinner,
she spends an hour washing the dishes and her
children. She goes to bed at 9:30 p.m.

In Pakistan, women spend 63 hours a week on housework. In Italy, 85 percent of mothers
70 who work outside the home also do all of the housework. Their husbands never help them.

This is only a small part of the information in the UN report. Will this report help change the life of women? Should there be a change?
75 **Are** women **supposed to** do the housework?   should
Should they work outside the home? Will the UN report help improve women's lives? Do they need improvement? Different people have different answers to these questions.
80 The family is changing **rapidly** in many   fast
societies. Any change in the family affects women. Any change in the lives of women affects the family and the society. Governments have already passed some laws affecting women be-
85 cause of the UN Decade for Women. The UN report will affect the changes now happening in the family and society.

A. Vocabulary

provides	prepared	published	official
agriculture	illiterate	training	supposed to
affect	rights	protected	domestic

1. What book company _____ this book?
2. Are you _____ for the big test tomorrow?
3. A _____ worker does a family's housework.
4. Hot and cold weather _____ people in different ways.
5. Firefighters need _____ before they can put out fires.
6. Caves _____ some people from the weather thousands of years ago.
7. In some countries, schools must give _____ exams at the end of the year. In others, each teacher writes an exam.
8. You are _____ come to class on time.

B. Vocabulary

share	frighten	illiterate	right
agriculture	training	protect	field
as well as	domestic	rapidly	typical

1. The children started fighting because one took more than his _____ of the cake.
2. Some movies _____ children so they can't sleep.
3. The world's population is increasing _____.
4. Marge helped her friend finish her work. This was _____ of Marge. She helps people a lot.
5. _____ is another word for *farming*.
6. Everyone has the _____ to enough food, a place to live, medical care, and an education.
7. People who can't read and write are _____.
8. There are some horses in the _____ behind the farmhouse.

C. Vocabulary Review
Match the words with their meaning.

1. relative _____
2. individual _____
3. population _____
4. increase _____
5. sociologist _____
6. method _____
7. shortage _____
8. distribute _____
9. disaster _____
10. decrease _____
11. figure _____

a. person who studies society
b. pass things out
c. get larger
d. get smaller
e. number
f. person
g. number of people in an area
h. way
i. natural resources
j. family member
k. frequent
l. not enough
m. terrible happening

HOURS IN A WOMAN'S DAY IN DEVELOPING COUNTRIES

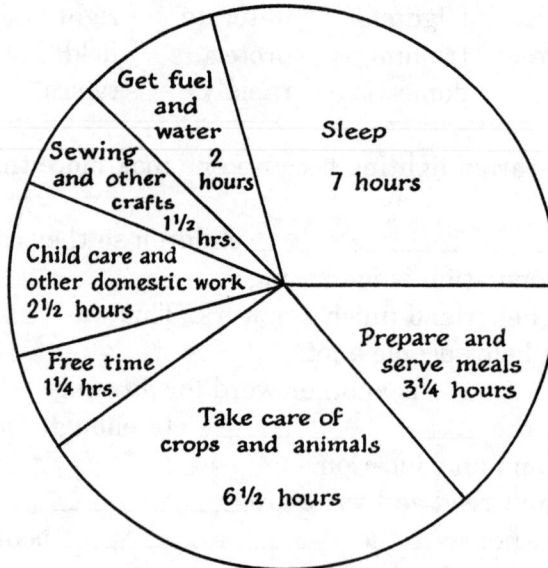

MEN'S AND WOMEN'S WORK IN AFRICA

	Percentage of Total Work in Hours	
	Men	Women
Cuts down forests, prepares fields	95	5
Turns the soil	70	30
Plants seeds and cuttings	50	50
Hoes and weeds	30	70
Gathers crops	40	60
Carries crops home	20	80
Stores crops	20	80
Processes food crops	10	90
Sells the extra crops	40	60
Carries water and fuel	10	90
Cares for domestic animals	50	50
Hunts	90	10
Feeds and cares for the family	5	95

SOURCE: UN Handbook on Women in Africa

D. Multiple Choice

Use the text and the charts to answer these questions.

1. In Africa, a village woman spends about _____ of her day farming.
   a. 1/4   b. 1/3   c. 1/2

2. The Decade for Women was organized by _____.
   a. UNICEF
   b. the World Health Organization
   c. the United Nations

3. _____ of all countries have official organizations to improve the life of women.
   a. All but 90 percent   b. Half   c. All but 10 percent

4. The average woman earns _____ the average man.
   a. more than   b. the same as   c. less than

5. _____ in the world are literate.
   a. More men than women
   b. More women than men
   c. About the same number of women and men

6. In Africa, _____ of the farm work is done by men.
   a. 80 percent   b. 50 percent   c. 20 percent

7. A typical woman in a developing country spends _____ collecting firewood daily.
   a. 1 hour   b. 2 hours   c. 1/2 hour

8. An African village man does about half of the _____.
   a. weeding   b. planting   c. hunting

9. Some _____ programs are changing because of the UN report.
   a. agricultural   b. water   c. industrial

10. In Africa, village _____ carry most of the crops, water, and fuel.
    a. men   b. women   c. children

E. Comprehension Questions

1. What does "women hold up half the sky" mean?
2. How many countries have laws to protect the rights of women?
3. Do you know any older women who are illiterate? If you do, why didn't they go to school?
4. Give a reason why some women work more hours than men.
5. Why do you think most Italian men don't help with the housework?
6. Is it easy to change the life of women in a society? Give a reason for your answer.
7. In your country, is the life of a young woman today different from the life of young women 50 years ago? Give two examples.

F. Main Idea

What is the main idea of this reading text? Write one or two sentences.

WORD STUDY

A. Scanning
Scan the reading text to find these answers. Write the answer and the number of the line where you found the answer.

1. What percentage of jobs are held by women?
2. What percentage of government jobs are held by women?
3. What percentage of countries have laws about equal pay?
4. In Africa, what percentage of farm work do women do?
5. How many hours a day do Pakistani women spend doing housework?
6. When was the Decade for Women?
7. What percentage of women have birth-control methods available?
8. What percentage of children in school are boys?

B. Word Forms
There is always a noun after an article. There might be an adjective before the noun.

Women do most of the **housework**.
An illiterate **person** cannot read or write.

	Verb	Noun	Adjective	Adverb
1.	publish	publication publisher		
2.	protect	protection	(un)protected protective	protectively
3.		(il)literacy	(il)literate	
4.	frighten	fright	frightening	frighteningly
5.		agriculture	agricultural	agriculturally
6.	provide	provision		
7.	train	training		
8.		type	typical	typically
9.	prepare	preparation		
10.	affect	effect	(in)effective	(in)effectively

1. *Newsweek* is a popular _____.
2a. The police provide _____ for the people in a country.

2b. Workers in dangerous jobs wear _____ clothing.
3. Few people are _____ in Japan. The educational system is very strong.
4. Ms. Baker had a _____ experience last night. A strange man was in her house when she got home from work late.
5. Very few people work in _____ in northern Russia. It is not an _____ area.
6a. The teachers will _____ food for the party.
6b. Explorers have to take a lot of _____ with them.
7. You have to _____ to be a police officer. _____ is necessary.
8. What _____ of student are you? Are you a _____ college student? A good student _____ studies a lot.
9. It is difficult to give a speech without _____.
10. Exercise has a good _____ on the muscles. If you exercise _____, you will have strong muscles.

C. Articles
Put articles in the blanks if they are necessary.

1. This is _____ old Chinese saying.
2. In 1975 _____ United Nations organized _____ Decade for Women.
3. Some of _____ news in _____ report is very good.
4. For example, 90 percent of all _____ countries now have _____ official organizations to improve _____ lives of _____ women.
5. Forty-one percent of _____ children in _____ school now are _____ girls.
6. _____ millions also work outside _____ home.
7. Sixty percent of _____ people who can't read are _____ women.
8. In _____ Africa, 60 percent of all agricultural work is done by _____ women.
9. In _____ Africa, this is _____ typical day for _____ village woman.
10. This is only _____ small part of _____ information in _____ UN report.

D. Connecting Words

Use the word **but** to connect a sentence from the second column with one from the first column. Make one complete sentence.

1. Some of the news in the report is good.   a. Only 41 percent go to school.
2. Half of the world's children are girls.   b. They use the most natural resources.
3. Many women work outside the home.   c. It can be increased only a little.
4. Rich countries have the fewest people.   d. Some of it is bad.
5. It is possible to increase the amount of farmland.   e. Most of it is salt water.
6. There is enough water in the world.   f. Their husbands don't help them with the housework.

E. Context Clues

1. The North Pole is in a cold **region** of the earth.
   a. temperature   b. frozen   c. area

2. Animals **such as** lions, hippopotamuses, and elephants live in Africa.
   a. for example   b. however   c. although

3. Babies are **tiny** when they are born.
   a. half grown   b. very small   c. ancient

4. Twenty-five is a **quarter** of one hundred.
   a. one-fourth   b. one-third   c. one-half

5. We get beef and milk from **cattle**.
   a. cows   b. sheep   c. goats

6. Miss Li **no longer** lives in Hong Kong. She moved to Taiwan.
   a. shorter   b. plans to   c. not any more

RAIN FORESTS

4

Tropical rain forests are found in the Amazon **region**, Central America, parts of Africa, and parts of South and Southeast Asia. These are thick forests with trees 45 meters high. These
5 huge trees have their first **branches** about 10 meters above the ground. Below the trees there is another level of plants — many kinds of smaller trees, bushes, and flowers.

Each level of the forest is its own world. The
10 lower level is protected by the trees above. The temperature and humidity (the amount of water or moisture in the air) stay about the same in the lower level. There is not much sunlight. In the upper level the sun, rain, and wind change the
15 temperature and humidity often.

It is amazing to find that there is an animal world in the upper level. There are monkeys, members of the cat family, birds, and insects **such as** **bees**, **butterflies**, and many kinds of
20 **flies**. There are also other animals that usually live on the ground — mice, **ants**, and even **earthworms**.

This upper level of the forest is thick with plant life because the trees are covered with
25 other plants. Most plants get **nutrients** from the ground through their **roots**. These plants in the upper level take their nutrients from the

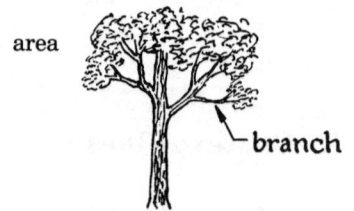

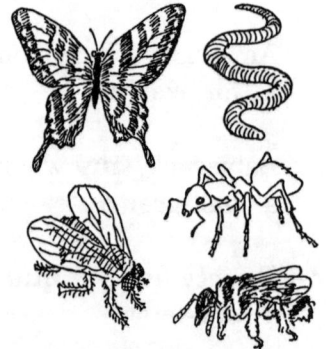

area

branch

such as = for example

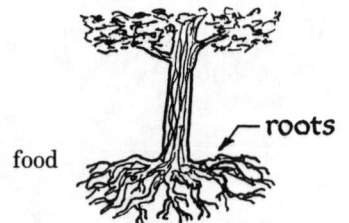

food

roots

82

trees they live on and from the other plants that die there.

30 The animals need "streets" so they can move along the upper level without going down to the ground. In order to travel in this upper level, they make paths along the branches of the trees. A researcher found a path that stretched
35 for 18 meters in one tree. One kind of **tiny** ant makes a path only 3 millimeters wide.

very small

Now **humans** are destroying the earth's tropical rain forests. About 100,000 square kilometers are being destroyed every year. About
40 one-fourth of the **destruction** comes from people cutting down trees for fuel. Another **quarter** is destroyed when people cut down trees to make grassland for their **cattle**. People cut down the rest of the trees so they can sell the wood or start
45 farms.

people

noun for *destroy*
1/4

The world needs more food, and it seems like a good idea to clear the rain forests and use the land for agriculture. Land that can support these huge, thick forests must be very rich in
50 nutrients. But it isn't. This is another surprising thing about rain forests.

Most of the land in tropical rain forests is very poor. The plants are able to live because of all the dead leaves and other parts of the plants
55 that fall to the ground. This carpet of dead plants provides nutrients for the living plants.

When the land is cleared for agriculture, there are **no longer** any plants left to die and provide nutrients for living plants. The **cycle** is
60 broken. Agriculture is not successful because the land cannot support it. Trees cannot grow again because the carpet of dead plants is gone. The land becomes empty and useless.

not any more
circle

Is this important? What does it matter to a
65 Japanese businessman, a French farmer, or an Arab student that people are destroying rain forests thousands of kilometers away?

Do you ever take medicine? Do you wear running shoes? Do you use envelopes when you
70 mail letters? Rain forests make these things possible.

Rain forests cover about 7 percent of the earth's area, but they have 100,000 kinds of plants, probably half of all the kinds of plants on
75 earth. Twenty percent of our different kinds of medicine comes from rain forests. The glue on an envelope and in shoes comes from tropical plants. Rain forests provide materials for hundreds of other products.

80 Rain forests are also very important to the world's climate. The Amazon rain forest alone receives about 30 to 40 percent of the total rainfall on the earth and produces about the same percentage of the world's oxygen (O). No
85 one knows how the decreasing size of the world's rain forests will affect the earth's climate.

Saving our rain forests is an international problem. One country or even a few countries cannot solve the problem alone. The nations of
90 the world must work together to find a **solution** before it is too late.   noun for *solve*

A. Vocabulary

bush	path	branch	such as
humans	quarter	no longer	solution
insects	tiny	level	roots
destruction	cattle	tropical	humidity

1. Flies, ants, and bees are examples of _____.
2. An insect is a _____ animal.
3. When students do well in their English classes, they move up to the next _____.
4. Masako had to leave the university and go home. She is _____ studying English.

5. _____ can work together to save rain forests.
6. Anne and Ken like to walk on a _____ along the river in the evening.
7. A _____ is part of a tree.
8. A _____ is a plant that grows lower than a tree.
9. _____ are cows.
10. Malaysia is a _____ country. The temperature and the _____ are both high there.
11. We must find a _____ to the problem of overpopulation.
12. The _____ of most plants are below the ground.

B. Vocabulary

fly	cycle	nutrients	path
ant	bee	moisture	region
oxygen (O)	such as	butterfly	earthworms
stretch	glue	quarter	no longer

1. The _____, _____, _____, and _____ are all insects.
2. A _____ is a circle.
3. Humans need to eat the right food in order to get the right _____.
4. Most of North Africa is a desert _____.
5. Carol needs some _____ to fix a broken plate.
6. People in Latin American countries _____ Ecuador, Peru, and Venezuela speak Spanish.
7. The Andes Mountains _____ from Colombia to Chile.
8. A _____ is one-fourth.
9. Most _____ live under the ground.
10. The amount of _____ in the air is called humidity.
11. _____ is necessary for life.

C. Vocabulary Review

rubber	ivory	treat	colony
attitude	although	average	metal
famine	industry	revolution	extended
nuclear	tribes	frightened	field

1. There are two kinds of families, _____ and _____.
2. The Indian _____ in the Americas came from Siberia.
3. Mr. Green has an excellent _____ about visiting a foreign country. He wants to learn everything about it that he can.
4. You don't have to like everybody, but you should _____ everyone the right way.
5. _____ Joe doesn't like to fly, he is going to Hawaii on his vacation.
6. Tires are made from _____.
7. Most _____ comes from elephants.
8. The United States was a British _____ until 1776. Then the American _____ made it a separate country.

D. True/False/No Information

_____ 1. Some rain forests are not in the tropics.

_____ 2. There is more change in weather in the upper level of a rain forest than in the lower.

_____ 3. In the upper level, some plants support the life of the other plants.

_____ 4. Plants get nutrients through their branches.

_____ 5. People destroy about 25,000 square kilometers of tropical rain forest every year so they can burn the wood.

_____ 6. The land in tropical rain forests is rich.

_____ 7. Tropical rain forest land can support forests, although it cannot support agriculture.

_____ 8. Material from rain forests is used to make cassette tapes.

_____ 9. Earthworms make paths on the branches of trees in rain forests.

_____ 10. There are rain forests in Brazil.

_____ 11. Rain forests have 100,000 kinds of plants.

E. Comprehension Questions

1. How is the weather in the lower level of a rain forest different from in the upper level?
2. Why is it amazing to find mice and earthworms in the upper level?
3. Where do most plants at the upper level get their nutrients?
4. Why do people cut down trees in rain forests?
5. Where do plants in the lower level get their nutrients?
6. What happens to the land when the trees are cut down?
7. Why are rain forests important to the world's climate?
8. What are some other reasons they are important to all of us?

F. Main Idea

1. Which sentence is the main idea for paragraph 3 (lines 16–22)?
2. Write your own sentence for the main idea of paragraph 12 (lines 72–79).

WORD STUDY

A. Noun Substitutes

Find each word and decide what it is a substitute for. It is usually a substitute for one word, but it might be for a whole sentence.

Example: In 1975, the United Nations organized the Decade for Women. In 1985, **it** published a report.

It is a substitute for **the United Nations**.

1. page 82, line   3   these
2.   27   their
3. page 83, line 28   they
4.   29   there
5.   30   they
6.   50   it
7.   50   this
8.   61   it
9.   64   this
10. page 84, line 73   they

B. Cause and Effect

Match the causes in the first column with the effects in the second column.

Cause	**Effect**
1. The upper level is thick with plants.	a. The weather doesn't change much in the lower level.
2. The trees are all cut down.	b. They make paths with branches.
3. A carpet of dead plants provides nutrients.	c. The land cannot support agriculture.
4. Animals want to travel in the upper level.	d. Tropical plants can live on poor land.
5. The lower level is protected by the upper level.	e. Tropical land becomes useless.

C. Articles
Put an article in each blank it if is necessary.

1. Below _____ trees there is another level of plants.
2. Each level of _____ forest is its own world.
3. _____ temperature and humidity (_____ amount of _____ water or _____ moisture in _____ air) stay about _____ same.
4. In _____ upper level, _____ sun, _____ rain, and _____ wind change _____ temperature and _____ humidity often.
5. It is amazing to find that there is _____ animal world in _____ upper level.
6. Most plants get _____ nutrients from _____ ground through their roots.
7. These plants in _____ upper level take their nutrients from _____ trees they live on and from _____ other plants that die there.
8. _____ researcher found _____ path that stretched for _____ 18 meters in one tree.
9. One kind of _____ tiny ant makes _____ path only 3 millimeters wide.

D. Word Forms

	Verb	Noun	Adjective	Adverb
1.		tropics	tropical	
2.		humidity	humid	
3.		moisture	moist	
4.		human humanity	(in)human	(in)humanly
5.	destroy	destruction	destructive	destructively
6.	solve	solution		
7.	endanger	danger	dangerous endangered	dangerously
8.		(in)ability (dis)ability	(un)able	ably
9.	(dis)appear	(dis)appearance		
10.	own	owner ownership		

1. Indonesia is in the _____.
2. It's hot and _____ today.

3. It's humid today and my skin is _____.
4a. _____ beings must work together to solve the world's problems.
4b. Some prisoners want to escape because the jailers treat them _____.
5. War is _____. It takes human life and _____ cities, villages, and agricultural land.
6. Dan finally figured out the _____ to his math problem.
7. The tropical rain forests of the world are _____. They are in _____ of being destroyed.
8a. Is the United Nations _____ to improve the life of women?
8b. Deafness and blindness are examples of a physical _____.
8c. The _____ to speak English is a problem for an international businessman.
9. The _____ of 100,000 square kilometers of rain forest a year is a serious problem.
10. Who is the _____ of that beautiful Mercedes Benz?

E. Context Clues

1. Tom has books, pencils, a radio, a cup, some cassettes, and several other **objects** on his desk.
   a. books   b. things   c. writing materials

2. There are plants that contain **poison** in both deserts and rain forests. If you eat one, you will get sick or even die.
   a. a kind of medicine
   b. a plant that can live on poor land
   c. something that can kill you

3. When the teacher gave 15 pages of homework, the students **protested**.
   a. said they didn't like it
   b. asked what the page numbers were
   c. asked for more

4. Don't dress up for the party tonight. Just wear your **ordinary** clothes.
   a. best   b. oldest   c. usual

GREENPEACE

5

The environment is everything around us, both natural and made by humans. A major problem in the world today is the destruction of the natural environment.

5   This is a **complicated** problem. We burn fuel, and this causes air pollution. We throw away millions of plastic bags, containers, toys, and other **objects**. These stay in the environment; they are not like paper or wood that slowly

10 disappear. We have made thousands of new chemicals. Factories that make or use chemicals always have chemical wastes. These are often poisonous, and they stay in the environment.

    Since 1945, several countries have been

15 testing **nuclear bombs** in the air and underground. The **explosions** in the air cause nuclear fallout. The fallout causes cancer and kills animals and people. Now there are nuclear power plants to make electricity. These produce dan-

20 gerous wastes and have accidents that can be very dangerous.

    The increase in the world's population means that we need more food. We also use more wood, metals, and other natural resources.

25   Individuals, governments, and international organizations worry about this problem and try to find solutions. Greenpeace is one

complicated ≠ simple, easy

things

🌐 🌐 🌐 🌐 🌐 🌐

nongovernmental, international organization that works to save the environment.

30   Greenpeace was organized in 1971 in Vancouver, British Columbia, on the west coast of Canada. It was organized because the United States was testing bombs on Amchitka Island in Alaska. These were American tests, but they
35 were very near Canada. When Greenpeace protested the tests, other people became interested. A year later, the testing was stopped because of the protests.

     Next, members of Greenpeace sailed to the
40 South Pacific to protest where France does nuclear testing on Moruroa, an island halfway between Chile and Australia. In 1973, the French stopped testing, but they started again in the 1980s. In 1985, a Greenpeace ship was in New
45 Zealand on its way to Moruroa again. Someone working for the French government put a bomb on the ship, and it sank. The explosion killed one man.

     Greenpeace also tries to save animals. Ev-
50 ery year hunters kill thousands of baby **seals** in Norway and Canada and sell the skins to make coats. Members of Greenpeace sail to the area and stand between the hunters and the seals. When ships hunt **whales**, Greenpeace sails to
55 the area, and then the members go in small boats between the whaling ships and the whales.

     Many countries put their chemical and nuclear wastes in the sea. Although the seas and oceans are huge, we are beginning to pollute
60 them with our wastes. Greenpeace is trying to protect the seas.

     Greenpeace believes that all **forms** of life   kinds
on earth depend on each other. All the forms of plant and animal life fit together in the environ-
65 ment. We need all of them. Greenpeace also believes that there is a limit to all of our natural resources. We need to take care of them and use

them carefully. We need to protect the earth for
our children.

70   Greenpeace works in two ways. It uses direct action; that is, it sends a ship directly to
where people are hunting whales or seals. It sails
into the area where France is testing bombs. Its
actions are always **nonviolent**; Greenpeace   peaceful
75 never fights or kills or hurts anyone. It always
works in a peaceful way.

When other people hear about this direct
action from newspapers, magazines, or television, they become worried about the problem
80 too. Then some of them try to make their government take action to solve the problem.

Greenpeace also uses indirect action. It
does research on chemicals, pollution, and nuclear wastes. It uses this research to try to make
85 governments change their laws.

Greenpeace also tries to educate people. It
works with other organizations and shares its
research and information. It makes films about
environmental problems. It gives lectures in
90 schools.

Where does Greenpeace get its money? Ordinary people in Europe, North America, Australia, and New Zealand give money. Some people also work for Greenpeace without receiving
95 any pay.

Greenpeace believes that we must all learn
to live in peace, not just with other humans, but
with all the beautiful animals on earth. We must
work now to protect the future of the earth, or it
100 may be too late.

A. Vocabulary

poisonous	nonviolent	depend on	explosion
nuclear	chemicals	whales	object
wastes	bombs	forms	direct

1. A _____ bomb is more dangerous than other bombs.
2. The USSR and the United States have thousands of nuclear _____.
3. Many organizations have _____ protests against nuclear bombs. They are peaceful.
4. A nuclear bomb causes a terrible _____.
5. Chemists have made thousands of new _____.
6. Some chemicals are _____.
7. The _____ from nuclear plants are dangerous.
8. Some _____ of life, such as dinosaurs, have disappeared from the earth.
9. Some organizations try to change the laws of the country. Others take _____ action to produce change.
10. Can I _____ you to take me to class every day? Will you ever forget to pick me up?

B. Vocabulary

form	ordinary	environment	protest
poisonous	complicated	object	explosion
whales	pollution	seals	wastes

1. _____ and _____ are animals.
2. Air _____ is a serious problem in Mexico City.
3. Factories pollute the _____.
4. _____ people in many countries _____ because their governments have nuclear bombs.
5. Doris had a strange _____ in her hand. I didn't know what it was.
6. Engineers have to solve _____ problems.

C. Vocabulary Review: Antonyms

Match the words that mean the opposite.

1.	warlike _____	a.	literate
2.	be supposed to _____	b.	slowly
3.	typical _____	c.	increase
4.	illiterate _____	d.	underpopulated
5.	individual _____	e.	peaceful
6.	no longer _____	f.	unusual
7.	rapidly _____	g.	rights
8.	huge _____	h.	shouldn't
9.	humid _____	i.	training
10.	decrease _____	j.	group
11.	overpopulated _____	k.	tiny
		l.	still
		m.	dry

D. Multiple Choice

1. The environment is _____.
   a. natural   b. made by people   c. both a and b

2. Poisonous chemicals pollute _____.
   a. air and water   b. wastes   c. explosions

3. Nuclear testing can cause _____.
   a. cancer   b. chemicals   c. both a and b

4. Greenpeace started as _____ organization.
   a. an American   b. a European   c. a Canadian

5. _____ tests nuclear bombs in the South Pacific.
   a. France   b. New Zealand   c. Australia

6. Greenpeace tries to protect _____.
   a. whaling ships that are far from the land
   b. seals that are killed for their skins
   c. people who have cancer from nuclear tests

7. Greenpeace believes that _____.
   a. all kinds of life depend on each other
   b. direct action is the only way to solve problems
   c. people cannot make their governments change

8. Greenpeace is _____.
   a. violent only when it is necessary
   b. violent if the hunters or whalers are violent
   c. never violent

9. Greenpeace gets its money from _____.
   a. ordinary people
   b. official government organizations
   c. other organizations

E. Comprehension Questions

1. Name two ways that we are destroying the environment.
2. Why are nuclear power plants dangerous?
3. Why are we using our natural resources faster than we used to?
4. Why was Greenpeace organized?
5. Why has Greenpeace gone to the South Pacific?
6. What are three things that Greenpeace tries to protect?
7. Why does Greenpeace take direct action?
8. How does Greenpeace try to educate people?
9. Do you think the pollution of the environment is serious? Give a reason for your answer.

F. Main Idea

1. Write a sentence that gives the main idea for paragraph 3 (lines 14–21).
2. Which sentence is the main idea of paragraph 8 (lines 49–56)?

WORD STUDY

A. Summarizing

Which sentence is the summary of the paragraph?

1. Paragraph 2 (lines 5–13)
   a. The pollution of the environment is a complicated problem.
   b. Chemicals and waste products pollute the earth.
   c. Factories pollute the environment.

2. Paragraph 11 (lines 70–76)
   a. Greenpeace uses nonviolent direct action.
   b. Greenpeace always works in a peaceful way.
   c. Greenpeace tries to stop nuclear testing.

3. Paragraph 14 (lines 86–90)
   a. Greenpeace makes films and gives lectures.
   b. Greenpeace shares its research.
   c. Greenpeace tries to educate people.

B. Connecting Words

Use **and** to connect a sentence from the first column with a sentence from the second column. Make one complete sentence, and use a comma before **and**.

1. Some chemicals are poisonous.
2. Nuclear explosions cause fallout.
3. There are more people in the world.
4. Greenpeace was organized to stop nuclear testing in Alaska.
5. Someone put a bomb on their ship.
6. Members of Greenpeace sail to the areas where men kill seals.
7. All forms of life fit together in the environment.

a. Fallout causes cancer.
b. We need all of them.
c. They stay in the environment.
d. The testing was stopped.
e. They stand between the men and the seals.
f. More people use more of our natural resources.
g. The explosion killed a man.

C. Two-Word Verbs

check in — tell the airline that you are there for the flight or tell the hotel you are there for your room

drop out — stop going to school

get through — finish

put back — put something where it was before or where it belongs

think over — think about carefully

1. I can't give you my answer right away. I have to _____ it _____. I'll tell you next week.
2. You have to _____ at the airport 45 minutes before your flight leaves.
3. Did you _____ with your homework yet?
4. David didn't finish college. He _____ after his second year.
5. Please _____ the food _____ in the refrigerator. Don't leave it out on the table.

D. Compound Words

Use a word from the first column and one from the second column to make a compound word.

1.	down	a.	work
2.	far	b.	land
3.	rain	c.	land
4.	fall	d.	hill
5.	half	e.	fall
6.	house	f.	ground
7.	grass	g.	off
8.	under	h.	out
9.	farm	i.	way

E. Context Clues

1. The **couple** next door to us has two children.
   a. two people   b. a husband and wife   c. a few

2. Stop talking **immediately**. This is a test.
   a. in a few minutes   b. right now   c. soon

3. Bob received a video tape recorder as a **gift** from his parents on his birthday.
   a. present   b. money   c. package

4. This textbook has a **variety** of exercises.
   a. vocabulary   b. few   c. several different kinds

5. We will have the class picnic **even though** the weather isn't very nice.
   a. The weather isn't nice, so we won't have the picnic.
   b. The weather isn't nice, but we'll have the picnic anyway.
   c. We won't have the picnic because the weather isn't nice.

Unit III

A MISHMASH (A HODGEPODGE)

The world is so full of a number of things,
I'm sure we should all be as happy as kings.

—Robert Louis Stevenson

THE ROADRUNNER

1

Beep Beep! People all over the world laugh at roadrunner cartoons, but the real bird is almost as funny as the cartoon.

5 The roadrunner lives in the desert region of the southwestern United States and northern Mexico. It is a bird, but it can only fly about as much as a chicken can. People gave it its name because they usually see it running across a road, but of course it spends more time among 10 the plants in the desert than it does on roads.

The roadrunner is quite a large bird—about 45 centimeters long and 25 high. People laugh when it runs because it looks so funny. It holds its head straight out in front and its tail sticks 15 straight out in back. It takes long steps and can run 30 kilometers an hour.

It eats an amazing **variety** of food. Although it eats plants **once in a while**, it is mostly a meat eater. Most of its diet is insects, 20 but it also catches birds, mice, and other small animals. It is even brave enough to catch tarantulas, **snakes**, and black widow **spiders**.

different kinds
sometimes

In the spring a male roadrunner begins looking for a female as a mate. When he finds 25 one, he gives her presents—a snake to eat or a twig (a tiny branch of a tree) to use in building a **nest**. Then they build their nest, the female lays eggs, and they raise their young.

Roadrunners can also become friendly with
30 people. One **couple** in Arizona feeds a pair of
roadrunners which come one at a time every day
and make a noise outside the window. If someone doesn't give the bird a piece of hamburger
immediately, the bird knocks on the window
35 with its **beak**.

wife and husband

right now

In early spring, the bird doesn't eat the
meat itself. It carries the meat to its nest to feed
its young. Later on it brings the young bird to
the house to beg for food itself.

40 When the woman whistles, the bird comes
running. When the man walks out the driveway,
the roadrunner walks along behind, like a dog or
cat.

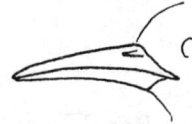

Another couple feeds a pair of roadrunners
45 which go right into the house. They will stand on
a chair or table and watch television, and they
seem really interested in what is happening on
the program. In the spring, the male sometimes
brings **gifts** to the couple—a leaf or twig for
50 building a nest, or an insect.

presents

In winter, when nighttime temperatures in
the desert can be 20°C colder than during the
day, the weather isn't warm until the middle of
the morning. The roadrunner has an unusual
55 way of keeping warm in this cold weather. In the
early morning, the roadrunner stands with its
back to the sun. It holds out its **wings** and lifts
the **feathers** on its upper back. There is a dark
spot on the skin under these feathers. This spot
60 collects heat from the sun and warms the bird's
body. The bird doesn't need to use a lot of energy
to keep warm the way most birds do.

Some people in Mexican villages use
roadrunner meat as medicine. They believe that
65 because roadrunners can eat poisonous animals
and not die, their meat should be good for human sickness.

A MISHMASH (A HODGEPODGE)

Maybe we shouldn't laugh at the roadrunner. **Even though** it looks funny when it runs,
70 it has developed a special way to keep warm, and it can eat poisonous animals. It can even make friends with humans. It fits into its environment very well, and it isn't important that it looks funny.

although

A. Vocabulary

variety	diet	male	female
mate	knock	driveway	feathers
even though	snakes	immediately	whistled
gift	special	stick out	couple

1. Some _____ are dangerous, but most are not.
2. A _____ connects the garage and the street.
3. There is a large _____ of food in a supermarket.
4. A woman is a _____, and a man is a _____.
5. The class is going to the museum _____ it is raining a little, and we have to walk.
6. The _____ in China is based on rice and vegetables.
7. Birds have _____.
8. Bill _____ for a taxi and one stopped.
9. Animals look for a _____ in spring.
10. Mr. and Mrs. Gorder are a married _____.
11. If you hear the fire alarm, leave the building _____.
12. Joan received a car from her parents as a _____ when she finished college.

B. Vocabulary

knock	programs	spot	once in a while
spider	wing	stick out	energy
diet	special	feather	immediately
even though	snake	nest	variety

1. An airplane has a _____ on each side so it can fly.
2. When I heard a _____ at the door, I went to answer it.
3. Mary watches television a lot, but she only goes to the movies _____.
4. An insect has six legs; a _____ has eight.
5. Don't _____ your tongue; it is very impolite.
6. Jean has a _____ on her new white jeans, and she can't get it out.
7. What television _____ do you like to watch?
8. We burn wood, gas, coal, and oil for _____.
9. Birds build a _____ in the spring.
10. There was a _____ meeting for new students during the first week of classes.

C. Vocabulary Review
Match the words with their definitions.

1. prepare _____
2. literate _____
3. bush _____
4. cattle _____
5. publish _____
6. region _____
7. nonviolent _____
8. cycle _____
9. be supposed to _____
10. such as _____
11. quarter _____
12. object _____

a. print and distribute books
b. should
c. one-fourth
d. get ready
e. for example
f. low plant
g. can read and write
h. area
i. tropical
j. cows
k. domestic
l. peaceful
m. circle
n. thing

D. True/False

_____ 1. The roadrunner runs around the desert looking for food.
_____ 2. Roadrunners live only in Mexico and the United States.
_____ 3. The female gives the male gifts in the spring.
_____ 4. A roadrunner is afraid of people and stays away from them.
_____ 5. This bird can learn to depend on people.
_____ 6. A big difference between daytime and nighttime temperatures is typical in the desert.
_____ 7. A roadrunner uses a lot of energy keeping warm in winter.
_____ 8. The roadrunner is a typical bird.

E. Comprehension Questions

1. What does a roadrunner eat?
2. Why does a male give gifts to the female?
3. Explain why the roadrunner is an unusual bird.
4. Why do people laugh at the roadrunner?
5. Explain how the roadrunner gets warm in the winter.
6. Do you think sick people will get better if they eat roadrunner meat? Explain your answer.
7. Do you think it is a good idea to feed wild animals? Give a reason.
8. Explain how a roadrunner fits into its environment.

F. Main Idea

Many paragraphs have a sentence that gives the main idea. It can be in different places in a paragraph.

1. Which sentence is the main idea of paragraph 4 (lines 17–22)?
2. Paragraph 10 (lines 51–62)?
3. Paragraph 11 (lines 63–67)?
4. Paragraph 12 (lines 68–74)?

WORD STUDY

A. Word Forms

Nouns are often used to describe other nouns. The meaning is different than when the adjective form of the same word is used.

> Cuba had a **literacy** program in the 1960s.
> A **literate** person can read and write.

In which sentence in this exercise does a noun describe another noun?

	Verb	Noun	Adjective	Adverb
1.		environment	environmental	environmentally
2.	complicate	complication	(un)complicated	
3.	pollute	pollution	(un)polluted	
4.	waste	waste	wasteful	wastefully
5.	explode	explosion	explosive	explosively
		explosive		
6.	depend (on)	(in)dependence	(in)dependent	(in)dependently
7.		(non)violence	(non)violent	(non)violently
8.	vary	variety	various	
		variation		
9.	specialize	specialty	special	especially
		specialist		
10.	know	knowledge	(un)known	(un)knowingly
			knowledgeable	knowledgeably

1. Water pollution is an _____ problem.
2a. A disease can cause _____ which make the person even sicker.
2b. This is a _____ problem, and I can't find the solution.
3. Are there any _____ rivers left in the world?
4. Some _____ products from factories can be reused.
5. A bomb _____ on a Greenpeace ship. The bomb was made of _____ .
6. Gandhi led India's _____ movement.
7. There has been a lot of _____ in Northern Ireland for several years.

A MISHMASH (A HODGEPODGE)

8a. The amount of rainfall in the Australian desert _____.
Some years there is only a little and other years a lot.

8b. A supermarket sells a large _____ of products.

8c. The true/false/no information exercises are a _____ on the true/false exercises.

9a. Most doctors _____ after they learn general medicine.

9b. Some words are _____ difficult to remember.

10a. Barbara is very _____ about birds. She knows a lot about them.

10b. The effect that cutting down rain forests will have on the world's climate is

_____.

10c. John would never _____ hurt his friend's feelings.

B. Prepositions

1. People all _____ the world laugh _____ roadrunner cartoons.
2. The roadrunner lives _____ the desert region _____ the United States and Mexico.
3. It spends more time _____ the plants _____ the desert than it does _____ roads.
4. Once _____ a while it eats plants.
5. In the spring a male roadrunner starts looking _____ a mate.
6. Roadrunners can also become friendly _____ people.
7. The birds come one _____ a time and make a noise _____ the window.
8. The bird knocks _____ the window _____ its beak.
9. These birds go right _____ the house.
10. They seem really interested _____ what is happening _____ the program.
11. _____ winter, nighttime temperatures _____ the desert can be 20°C colder than _____ the day.
12. _____ the early morning, the roadrunner stands _____ its back ____ the sun.

C. Summarizing
Which sentence is the summary?

1. Paragraph 4 (lines 17–22)
   a. It eats a large variety of food.
   b. It eats both plants and meat.
   c. It eats a large variety of food, both plants and meat.

2. Paragraphs 6 through 9 (lines 29–50)
   a. Roadrunners follow people, ask for food, and watch television.
   b. Roadrunners can become friendly with people.
   c. Roadrunners sometimes bring gifts to people.

3. Paragraph 10 (lines 51–62)
   a. Temperatures are much colder at night than during the day.
   b. A roadrunner has an unusual way to keep warm in winter.
   c. A roadrunner collects heat from the sun through a black spot on its back.

D. Connecting Words

Connect a sentence from the first column with one from the second column using **even though**.

1. A roadrunner fits into its environment.
2. Greenpeace tries to stop nuclear testing.
3. Rain forests cannot support agriculture.
4. Population is increasing rapidly.

5. Women do most of the domestic work.

a. They have 100,000 kinds of plants.
b. It is sometimes dangerous.
c. They work outside the home.
d. Half the world's women have birth-control methods available.
e. It looks funny when it runs.

E. Context Clues

1. The television program I watched last night was **boring**. It was so slow that I turned it off.
   a. uninteresting   b. interesting   c. exciting

2. When the beautiful young woman saw Dracula coming toward her, she was **terrified**.
   a. very happy   b. very frightened   c. very unhappy

3. Some people are afraid of insects, but most of them can't **harm** you.
   a. hurt   b. run away from   c. fly onto

A MISHMASH (A HODGEPODGE)

4. After the passengers **boarded** the plane, they put their bags under the seats and fastened their seatbelts.
   a. left   b. saw   c. got on

5. If you want to buy some stamps, you'd better **rush**. The post office closes in 5 minutes.
   a. walk   b. hurry   c. get some money

AFRAID TO FLY

Have you ever flown? Did you fly to another country to study English? How do you feel about flying?

People who have to fly all the time for
5 business usually find it **boring**. People who fly only once in a while are excited. However, some people feel only **terror** when they **board** an airplane. They suffer from a phobia, an illogical fear.

10   If you are afraid of poisonous spiders, it is logical. If you are afraid of all spiders, even **harmless** ones, this is a phobia because it is illogical. Some people have phobias about heights, being shut up in a small area, or being
15 in a large open area. It is not logical to be afraid of these things when there is no danger, but a phobia is not logical.

Fear of flying is another phobia. We always hear about a plane crash, but we don't hear
20 about the millions of flights every year that are safe. Riding in a car is thirty times more dangerous than flying, but most of us are not afraid every time we get into a car. It is not logical to be afraid of flying, but research shows that about
25 12 percent of people have this fear.

People with a phobia about flying are afraid for one or more reasons. They are afraid of heights. They avoid high places, and if they are

boring ≠ interesting

terror = strong fear / board = get on

not dangerous

112

in a high-rise building, they don't look out the
30 windows.

They might be afraid of being in an enclosed
place like an elevator or a **tunnel** on a highway.
When they get on an airplane, they can't get out
until the end of the flight, and the flight might
35 last several hours.

Maybe they are afraid of the crowds and all
the noise and people **rushing** around at an air-   hurrying
port. This especially bothers older people.

Some people are afraid of the unknown.
40 They don't understand the technology of flying
and can't believe that a huge airplane can stay
up in the air.

Others are afraid of **loss** of control. They   noun for *lose*
need to control every situation they are in. When
45 they drive a car, they have some chance of avoid-
ing an accident. In a plane, they have no control
over anything. It **terrifies** them to give up con-   verb for *terror*
trol to the pilot and the rest of the crew.

For some people, a fear of flying is not
50 important because they don't really need to fly.
But what about someone who works for an international company? What about an enter-
tainer who has to sing in twenty different places
in a month? These people have to fly if they want
55 to continue in their profession.

There is help for these people. There are
special classes in which people learn how to
control their fear. They probably can't lose it,
but they can learn to control it. Then they can fly
60 when they need to, even though they probably
won't enjoy it.

The class visits an airport and learns how
airplane traffic is controlled and how planes are
kept in safe condition. A pilot talks about flying
65 through storms, the different noises an airplane
makes, and air safety in general.

The class learns to do relaxation exercises,
and the people talk about their fear.

Next, the class listens to tape recordings of
70 a takeoff and landing, and later the people ride in
a plane on the ground around the airport. Finally they are ready to take a short flight.

The instructors of these classes say that
between 80 and 90 percent of the people who
75 take them are successful. They still have their
phobia, but they learn to control their fear.

A. Vocabulary

terror	height	fear	rush
situation	crew	takeoff	tunnel
harm	board	phobia	enclosed

1. The people who work on airplanes and ships are called the _____.
2. Tom found himself in a difficult _____ and he didn't know what to do.
3. A _____ is an illogical fear of something.
4. _____ is a very strong word for *fear*.
5. _____ is the feeling you have when you are afraid.
6. When you are in a hurry, you _____.
7. Some dogs bite, but most of them won't _____ anyone.
8. Passengers check in at the airport. Then they _____ the plane.
9. After _____, the airplane crew usually brings around drinks and food.
10. Some people become terrified when they are in an _____ space.
11. What is the _____ of the tallest building in your city?

B. Vocabulary

boring	suffer	tunnels	losses
terrified	profession	bother	board
last	instructor	crash	avoid

1. Many people in Africa _____ from hunger.
2. Anne was _____ when she saw the car coming straight at her.

3. What is your _____? Are you a doctor?
4. Ali's company suffered so many _____ that he went out of business.
5. An _____ is a teacher.
6. A plane _____ usually kills a lot of people.
7. David's composition had very few mistakes, but it was _____ to read.
8. When you have a cold, try to _____ giving it to your friends.
9. There are several _____ under the rivers. They connect Manhattan Island to the other parts of New York.
10. Please don't _____ me now. I'm busy.
11. How long does this class _____? An hour or less?

C. Vocabulary Review

Cross out the word that does not belong with the other two.

1. stick out, diet, cut down
2. once, couple, pair
3. feather, knock, wing
4. plateau, cloud, mountain
5. even, even though, although
6. often, sometimes, once in awhile
7. pollution, surroundings, environment
8. three-quarters, two-thirds, 40 percent
9. ant, butterfly, bee
10. relatives, females, ancestors

D. Multiple Choice

1. _____ usually think flying is boring.
   a. People who fly once in a while
   b. People who fly often
   c. People who have a phobia about flying

2. A phobia is _____.
   a. harmful   b. illogical   c. chemical

3. About _____ percent of people are afraid to fly.
   a. 6   b. 12   c. 15

4. A person with a fear of enclosed places doesn't like _____.
   a. walking on a path   b. high places   c. being in a tunnel

5. _____ especially bother old people.
   a. Crowds at airports   b. High-rise buildings   c. Spiders

6. A fear of flying is not important to some people because _____.
   a. they are entertainers
   b. they don't need to fly
   c. they can take a class about flying

7. The instructor of a class for people who are afraid of flying _____.
   a. explains about airplane crashes
   b. learns to relax
   c. takes them to an airport

8. More than _____ percent of people who take these classes are successful.
   a. 12   b. 80   c. 90

E. Comprehension Questions

1. Have you ever flown? If you have, when was the last time you flew?
2. What are some phobias? Do you have any phobias?
3. Why are we not afraid when we get into a car?
4. Give four reasons people are afraid of flying.
5. Give four examples of people who need to fly.
6. What do people learn in a class for people who are afraid of flying? Tell three things.
7. The class learns how airplane traffic is controlled. How does this help people who are afraid of flying?
8. Why does the class learn about the different noises a plane makes?
9. How do relaxation exercises help the people in the class?

F. Main Idea

1. Which sentence is the main idea of paragraph 8 (lines 39–42)?
2. Paragraph 11 (lines 56–61)?
3. Write a sentence for the main idea of the last paragraph.

WORD STUDY

A. Word Forms: Adverbs

Adverbs describe verbs. They also describe adjectives or other adverbs. Many adverbs end in **-ly**, for example **badly** and **nicely**. But there are a few adjectives that also end in **-ly**, for example, **friendly** and **lovely**. There are also some common adverbs that do not end in **-ly**, such as **fast** and **hard**.

Please return to the office **immediately**.
Your solution to this math problem is **completely** wrong.
Ali worked **especially** hard today.
Ann is a **friendly** person.
Mike works **hard** at his job.

Sometimes an adverb or an adverbial phrase describes the whole sentence.

Most importantly, you must hand in a report of the meeting by tomorrow morning.
Ordinarily, the class finishes at 2:00. Today it lasts until 2:30 because we have a special lecture.

	Verb	Noun	Adjective	Adverb
1.	poison	poison	poison poisonous	
2.	avoid	avoidance	(un)avoidable	(un)avoidably
3.	bore	boredom		boredly boringly
4.	suffer	suffering		
5.	fear	fear	fearful fearless	fearfully fearlessly
6.	lose	loss	lost	
7.	terrify	terror terrorist	terrified terrifying	

1. Mr. Smith _____ his rich wife so he could have all her money.

2. It is _____ for beginning students to make mistakes in English.

3. Students in an English program do not suffer from _____.
   They are too busy studying. They don't get _____.
4. There is a lot of _____ in poor countries.
5. Superman is _____.
6. The Student Union has a _____ and Found office. If you
   are lucky, you might go there and find something that you left in the
   cafeteria by mistake.
7. Two _____ with a bomb hijacked an airplane and made the
   pilot fly to Beirut. The passengers were _____.

B. Summarizing

Write a sentence to summarize each of these paragraphs. Number 2 will have a
long sentence. Write a sentence with only the most important idea for numbers
1 and 3.

1. Paragraph 3 (lines 10–17)
2. Paragraphs 5, 6, 7, 8, and 9 (lines 26–48)
3. Paragraph 10 (lines 49–55)

C. Articles

Write an article in the blanks if one is necessary.

1. _____ people who have to fly all _____ time for _____ business
   usually find it boring.
2. However, some people feel only _____ terror when they board _____
   airplane.
3. They suffer from _____ phobia, _____ illogical fear.
4. If you are afraid of _____ poisonous spiders, this is logical.
5. Some people have _____ phobias about _____ heights, being shut up
   in _____ small area, or being in _____ large open area.
6. We always hear about _____ plane crash, but we don't hear about
   _____ millions of _____ flights every year that are safe.
7. They avoid _____ high places, and if they are in _____ high-rise
   building, they don't look out _____ windows.
8. They might be afraid of being in _____ enclosed place like _____
   elevator or _____ tunnel on _____ highway.

9. When they get on _____ airplane, they know they can't get out until _____ end of _____ flight, and _____ flight might last several hours.
10. Maybe they are afraid of _____ crowds and all _____ noise and _____ people rushing around at _____ airport.

D. Connecting Words
Find a sentence in the second column that goes with a sentence in the first column. Connect the two sentences with **and**, **but**, or **even though**.

1. Businessmen are bored with flying.
2. A roadrunner fits well into its environment.
3. Kingsley traveled in West Africa by herself.
4. The boat was caught in a bad storm.
5. Scott reached the South Pole.

a. She was a Victorian woman.
b. It looks funny.
c. Amundsen had gotten there first.
d. People who don't fly very often find it exciting.
e. It sank.

E. Context Clues

1. The president has to **analyze** the situation carefully before he can make a decision, so he needs to get every piece of information that he can.
   a. think carefully about every detail of a situation
   b. get a general idea of the main situation
   c. find out why something happened

2. Thomas Edison **invented** the electric light.
   a. figured out
   b. discovered
   c. made the first one

3. A journalist **interviewed** a couple who feed a roadrunner. After she had talked to the couple, she wrote an article about the interview for a magazine.
   a. asked questions on a subject
   b. gave a lecture
   c. went to visit

A MISHMASH (A HODGEPODGE)

4. My neighbor's child says he did not take the money that was on my table. I believe him because he is very **honest**.
   a. usually tells the truth
   b. doesn't usually steal
   c. tells the truth and never steals

5. It is hard to stay **calm** when your basketball team needs only one point to win, and there are just 30 seconds left in the game.
   a. unexcited
   b. complicated
   c. explosive

HANDWRITING ANALYSIS

3

Ellen Shepherd is a handwriting analyst. The author asked her questions about this interesting subject in an interview. In this report of the interview, P.A. stands for the author's
5 name and E.S. are Ms. Shepherd's initials.

P.A.: I've heard about handwriting analysis, but I don't know much about it. Could you explain what it is?

E.S.: It's a scientific system which analyzes
10 someone's handwriting. The analysis shows the person's personality and character—what kind of person this individual is. The handwriting shows if the person is honest or dishonest, gets angry easily or stays **calm**, has a good memory

                                       calm ≠ excited or angry

15 or forgets easily. We can tell when people's feelings have a strong effect on their thinking, or if they usually think logically. We can tell if the person has a lot of friends and likes to spend time with them, or if he likes to be alone most of
20 the time. We can even tell when people are shy. They're so afraid of other people that they spend most of their time alone when they'd really like to be with others.

P.A.: That's amazing! But you've given a list of
25 opposites. Most people are somewhere in the

122

middle, or they act differently in different situations. For example, someone might get very angry about something important but just a little angry about something else. Can you tell 30 about degrees of anger or laziness or other characteristics?

E.S.: Yes, we can. We can score this person from one to ten on how angry she gets. We can also tell if she often feels angry inside even though she 35 appears to be calm. We can do the same thing for other feelings and characteristics. For example, we can tell to what degree people work carefully, or if they're sometimes lazy and careless.

P.A.: How do you do this analysis?

40 E.S.: First I have them write about two pages on unlined paper. Then I look at how they make each stroke of the letters.

P.A.: What's a stroke?

E.S.: In general, a stroke is the part of a letter 45 that leaves or returns to the base line. The cross on a *t* and the dot on an *i* are also strokes.

P.A.: Do you mean you can look at the way I cross my *t*'s and dot my *i*'s and tell what kind of person I am?

50 E.S.: (Laughing) Of course not. I have to analyze the whole two pages of writing. I divide the parts of the letters into zones. Letters like *f*, *h*, and *l* go into the upper zone. This zone shows people's imagination, ideas, and how they think about 55 the future.

All letters have parts in the middle zone. This zone shows how people think and feel about

the present and reality, and their feelings about other people.

60   Letters like *f*, *g*, and *p* go into the lower zone. This zone shows how people feel about the past, if they're quick to take action, and what their biological needs are. For example, food is very important to some people. Others are not
65 interested in food at all, as long as they have enough to eat.

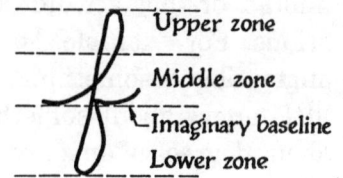

P.A.: It's hard for me to believe that you can get all that information about a person just from handwriting.

70 E.S.: People talk about body language. The way you hold and move your body shows a lot about what kind of person you are. For example, if you hold your head down a lot, you're probably shy. The way you write is much more complicated
75 than the way you hold your body, so it gives a lot more information. Research shows this.

P.A.: Is handwriting analysis something new?

E.S.: An American teacher, M.N. Bunker, invented this system in 1913, but even the ancient
80 Chinese, Greeks, and Romans noticed that personality showed in handwriting. In the 1600s an Italian started to develop a system, and 200 years later the French were working on one. Today in Europe, anyone who is studying to be a
85 teacher or a psychologist has to study handwriting analysis.

P.A.: Who uses handwriting analysis?

E.S.: Some companies use it when they hire people to work for them. They want to know if
90 they'll be good, honest workers. Police use it to try to understand criminals better. Sometimes

Upper zone
Middle zone
Imaginary baseline
Lower zone

an individual wants an analysis to help decide what kind of job is best for him or her. These are just a few examples.

95 P.A.: There's something else I'm wondering about. When we go to school, we all learn to write the same way.

E.S.: I know what you're thinking, but everyone writes differently. There is about one chance in
100 68 trillion that two people will write exactly the same.

P.A.: And there aren't even that many people in the world! So far we've talked about European languages and our alphabet. What about analyz-
105 ing Arabic or Japanese?

E.S.: I don't think anyone has developed a system for any other alphabets, but since everybody writes differently, handwriting analysis should work for any alphabet.

110 P.A.: This has been very interesting, and I've learned a lot. Thanks for explaining it all to me.

E.S.: Thank you for interviewing me. If anything is unclear, just call me.

A. Vocabulary

honest	score	exactly	system
shy	analyze	interviews	initials
character	stroke	biological	psychologist

1. What _____ do you need on the TOEFL test in order to enter Harvard University?
2. No two individuals are _____ alike, not even twins.

3. Companies try to hire _____ people. They try to hire people with a good _____.
4. England has one _____ of government. The USSR has another.
5. Dr. Barnes is a child _____. He helps children who have problems in their lives.
6. Susan is five years old and very _____. She hides behind her mother when people talk to her.
7. Television news programs often have _____ with famous people.
8. It is nice to have a lot of money, but it isn't a _____ need.
9. Dr. Gomez will use her computer to _____ her research.

B. Vocabulary

stand for	personality	strokes	calm
honest	invented	initials	zones
as long as	hire	imagination	system

1. The _____ of the author of this book are P.A.
2. Mike has a very nice _____. He is friendly to everyone.
3. Some people will travel anywhere _____ they don't have to fly.
4. Japanese write with a lot of short _____.
5. Ms. Davis tried to stay _____ even though she was very worried about her daughter.
6. Cities in many countries have _____ for the postal system. Each one has a number.
7. What does U.S. _____? The United States.
8. The Bakers are going to _____ someone to do their domestic work.
9. The person who _____ the typewriter had a wonderful idea.
10. A handwriting analyst can tell if a person has a good _____.

A MISHMASH (A HODGEPODGE)

C. Vocabulary Review

branches	level	root	earthworms
stretch	glue	moisture	nutrients
flies	direct	whale	seal
spot	snakes	whistle	gift

1. I have to _____ these papers together.
2. It bothers me when _____ come around the food at a picnic.
3. Some _____ are poisonous. _____ are not, even though they have a similar shape.
4. Maria is at the highest _____ in the English program.
5. When we eat a carrot, we are eating the _____ of the plant.
6. Eskimos eat _____ and _____ meat.
7. Some food provides more _____ than other food.
8. Leaves grow on the _____ of trees.
9. Some people can _____ songs very well.
10. Desert animals don't drink much water. They get it from the _____ in plants they eat.

D. True/False

_____ 1. The analysis of handwriting shows a person's character.
_____ 2. An analyst can tell if a person is afraid to try new things.
_____ 3. An analyst can score a person on how logically he thinks.
_____ 4. The analyst looks at about two lines of writing.
_____ 5. The letter y goes into the upper zone.
_____ 6. The upper zone shows if a person can draw or write well.
_____ 7. The lower zone shows how people feel about the present.
_____ 8. A teacher invented a system to analyze handwriting.
_____ 9. Handwriting analysis can help you choose a profession.
_____ 10. It is probably possible to analyze Chinese handwriting.

E. Comprehension Questions

1. Tell three things that a handwriting analyst can find out from a person's handwriting.
2. What does *shy* mean?
3. How does the analyst analyze the writing?
4. What zones is the letter *b* in?
5. What does the middle zone show?
6. What is body language?
7. How could handwriting analysis help you choose a profession?
8. What area of the world takes handwriting analysis the most seriously?
9. Do you think an analyst can tell a people's character from their handwriting? Give your reasons.
10. Do you think handwriting analysis is a science? Give your reasons.

F. Main Idea

1. Write a sentence for the main idea for paragraph 11 (lines 50–55).
2. Write a sentence for the main idea for paragraph 15 (lines 70–76).
3. Write a sentence for the main idea for paragraph 21 (lines 98–101).

A MISHMASH (A HODGEPODGE)

WORD STUDY

A. Word Forms: Active and Passive

In an active sentence, the subject performs (does) the action.

> The **interviewer** asked several questions.

In a passive sentence, the subject receives the action. The passive is formed with a form of **be** and a past participle. Sometimes the person (the agent) who performed the action is included in the sentence after the word **by**. The agent is not included if it is unknown or unimportant. Sometimes everyone knows who the agent is, so it is not necessary to name it.

> Several **questions** were asked by the interviewer.
> My **car** was stolen last night. (I don't know who stole it.)
> **Society** is studied so that **it** can be better understood. (The people who study society are not important in this sentence.)
> **Cars** are made in factories. (Everyone knows they are made by people.)

	Verb	Noun	Adjective	Adverb
1.	instruct	instruction	instructive	
		instructor		
2.		(dis)honesty	(dis)honest	(dis)honestly
3.	systematize	system	(un)systematic	(un)systematically
4.	imagine	imagination	(un)imaginative	(un)imaginatively
5.	invent	invention	inventive	
		inventor		
6.	interview	interview		
		interviewer		
7.	characterize	character	(un)characteristic	(un)characteristically
		characteristic		
8.		psychology	psychological	psychologically
		psychologist		
9.	beg	beggar		
10.	depend (on)	dependability	(un)dependable	dependably

Write the correct word form in the blanks, including active/passive forms.

1a. The lecture on safe driving was very _____.

1b. The students _____ to arrive on time the first day of classes.

2. _____ is an important characteristic for someone working in a bank.

3. Pat organizes her work _____. She can do more work in less time when she _____ it.

4. The mystery program I watched last night was very _____. I didn't know how it was going to end until the last minute.

5a. A computer programmer has to be _____ in order to write a good computer program.

5b. The telephone _____ by Alexander Graham Bell.

6. The Minister of Health didn't like some of the questions that the _____ asked him. He _____ by a foreign journalist.

7. Marge started a fight with her sister last night. This was very _____ of her because she is usually nice to her.

8. Barbara is going to study _____. Then she will work with people who have _____ problems.

9. Dan _____ his friend to lend his his car.

10. Mr. Thompson is a _____ person. If he says he will do something, you know that he will. You can _____ him.

B. Two-Word Verbs

pick someone up — go somewhere with your car and get someone

stand for — U.S. stands for the United States, for example

see off — go with someone to the airport, for example, when he or she is going to leave

clean up — clean the house after a party, for example, or after some children had a lot of toys out

help out — help

1. UN _____ the United Nations.

2. Tom had a big party. Afterward, he had to _____ the house. Three of his friends stayed to _____.

3. Ali studied at New York University for 5 years. When he left, 20 people went to the airport to _____ him _____.

4. Let's go to the party together. I'll _____ you _____ at 9:00.

A MISHMASH (A HODGEPODGE)

C. Prepositions
Put the right prepositions in the blanks.

1. The author asked her questions _____ this interesting subject _____ an interview.
2. I don't know much _____ it.
3. We can tell when people's feelings have a strong effect _____ their thinking.
4. We can tell if the person has a lot _____ friends and likes to spend time _____ them.
5. You've given a list _____ opposites.
6. Most people are somewhere _____ the middle, or they act differently _____ different situations.
7. We can score this person _____ one _____ ten _____ how angry she gets.
8. We can do the same thing _____ other feelings and characteristics.
9. Then I look _____ how they make each stroke _____ the letters.
10. _____ general, a stroke is the part _____ a letter that leaves or returns _____ the base line.

D. Noun Substitutes
What does each noun substitute stand for?

1. page 122,   line   2   her   _____
2.   line   8   it   _____
3.   line   15   we   _____
4.   line   16   their   _____
5.   line   19   he   _____
6. page 123,   line   33   she   _____
7. page 124,   line   64   others   _____
8.   line   76   this   _____
9.   line   83   one   _____
10. page 125,   line   93   him or her   _____

E. Context Clues

1. New York City is famous for its **skyscrapers**. It has more than any other city in the world.
   - a. art museums
   - b. wide streets
   - c. tall buildings

2. Carol is only eight years old, but she loves to draw buildings. She wants to be an **architect** when she grows up.
   - a. artist
   - b. person who plans new buildings
   - c. engineer

3. Mr. Miners is a **pleasant** teacher. He is friendly and helpful to all his students and to the other teachers.
   - a. nice
   - b. busy
   - c. new

4. Research shows that seatbelts help **prevent** serious injuries in accidents.
   - a. stop something before it happens
   - b. have fewer accidents
   - c. hold the person in the seat

5. In the modern world, people **communicate** by telephone, radio, television, and computer.
   - a. talk to each other
   - b. give and receive information
   - c. get the world's news

SKYSCRAPERS

4

When people think of skyscrapers, they think of New York, the city with the most high-rise buildings in the world. There is no other city like New York, and this is because of its great
5 buildings that reach up into the sky.

It comes as a surprise then, to learn that Chicago, not New York, is the home of the skyscraper. The first high-rise building was built in Chicago in 1884, and it was nine **stories** high.
10 This is not tall compared with today's buildings, but it was the first building over six stories. There were no tall buildings before that because the needed technology didn't exist.

For centuries, the tallest buildings were
15 made of stone. The lower walls had to be thick enough to support the upper ones. If the building was very high, the lower walls had to be very thick.

Early in the nineteenth century, engineers
20 developed **iron frames for bridges**. In the 1880s, **architects** started using iron and steel frames to support the walls of buildings. The buildings did not need thick walls to hold up the upper stories, so the buildings could be much
25 taller.

There were other advantages to these steel frames. The building walls were thinner and could have more windows, which made the

floors

people who design buildings

133

rooms much more **pleasant**. With thin lower
30　walls, there was room for stores and offices on
the ground floor. It was also faster to build with
an iron and steel frame than with stone.

　　However, there was still one problem. How
would people get up to the top stories in a 10-
35　story building? We all know what the solution
was—the elevator. Elisha Otis invented the elevator and first showed it to the public in 1853.
By the 1880s, there were elevators run by electricity which were fast and light enough to use in
40　skyscrapers. They were developed just at the
right time.

　　There were other problems that architects
and engineers who built high-rise buildings had
to solve. They had to figure out a way to get
45　water to all the floors. They had to prevent the
buildings from moving in the wind. **In addition**, they wanted to make them as beautiful as
possible.

　　At the time that architects first started de-
50　signing and building high-rise buildings, thousands of immigrants were entering the United
States from Europe. They all needed a place to
live. Cities were growing fast, and tall buildings
meant many more people could live in a small
55　area, so people started building skyscrapers in
cities across the United States.

　　Over the years, the problems connected
with high-rise buildings were solved. Buildings
got taller and taller. In 1909, a 50-story building
60　was built in New York, and in 1913, one with 60
floors. In 1931, the Empire State Building in
New York was finished; it was 102 stories high.
This was the tallest building in the world until
1970, when the World Trade Center was built,
65　again in New York. It has 110 floors. Then the
Sears Building was built in Chicago in 1974. It
also has 110 stories, but it is taller than the
World Trade Center.

nice

and

A MISHMASH (A HODGEPODGE)

Other countries were building skyscrapers
70   too. In Europe, the center of many cities was
destroyed by bombs during World War II. The
city planners rebuilt many of the buildings exactly as they had been. In addition, they included
high-rises in their plans. Most European cities
75   today are a mixture of old and modern buildings.

Tokyo did not have tall buildings for a long
time because of **earthquakes**. Then engineers   movements of the earth
figured out how to keep a high-rise standing
during an earthquake. Today there are many tall
80   buildings in Tokyo. In fact, there are tall buildings in cities throughout the world. As the population of cities increases, the number of high-
rises increases because they take less surface
space.

85   And what about the future? Architects say
there is no limit to the height a building can be.
An engineer in New York is designing a 150-floor
building. An architect in Chicago has drawings
of a 210-story building.

90   We have the technology for these buildings,
but do we need them or want them? With the
invention of computers, a company doesn't need
to have all its offices in one huge building. People
can **communicate** by computer from offices   exchange information
95   spread out all over the city, or even from their
homes. And do we want 200-story buildings? Do
people want to work and live that far above the
ground? The architects and engineers who are
planning these new skyscrapers have to think
100   about these questions, or they may build buildings that no one will use.

A. Vocabulary

skyscraper	advantages	frame	prevent
immigrants	designs	communicate	exist
compare	pleasant	in addition	connects

1. When we _____ Canadian English to English in the United States, we see that there are not many differences.
2. There are many _____ to learning English because it is an international language.
3. A high-rise building is also called a _____.
4. A driveway _____ the garage with the street.
5. Thousands of _____ arrive in Australia from Asia and Europe every year.
6. It is possible to _____ many forest fires that people start.
7. In some skyscrapers, the walls are made of a steel _____ and glass.
8. An architect _____ buildings.
9. Greenpeace protests nuclear testing. _____ , it tries to protect the seas.

B. Vocabulary

pleasant	mixture	compare	spread
exist	architect	story	earthquake
advantage	communicate	prevent	public

1. Hot chocolate is a _____ of chocolate, sugar, and milk.
2. We've had _____ weather lately. It has been warm and sunny.
3. In the future, we will _____ with computers even more than we do now.
4. An _____ in Turkey destroyed several villages.
5. Dinosaurs do not _____ anymore.
6. A famous _____ designed the whole city of Brasilia.
7. The children _____ their toys all over the floor and then went to watch television.

A MISHMASH (A HODGEPODGE)

8. Another word for the floor of a building is _____.
9. The lecture on modern architecture tonight is open to the _____. Anyone can go.

C. Vocabulary Review

Match the words with the definitions.

1. colony _____   a. better
2. interior _____   b. half of the earth
3. border _____   c. get away from
4. delay _____   d. place that belongs to another
                                          country
5. blind _____   e. to the shore
6. superior _____   f. line between two countries
7. escape _____   g. can't see
8. hemisphere _____   h. remote
9. ashore _____   i. inside
10. blizzard _____   j. sled
                                      k. bad winter storm
                                      l. wait

D. Multiple Choice

1. The first skyscraper was built in _____.
   a. Chicago   b. New York   c. Tokyo

2. Skyscrapers did not exist before 1884 because _____.
   a. steel did not exist
   b. people didn't have the necessary technology
   c. there were not enough immigrants to live in them

3. Architects got the idea of using iron and steel frames for buildings from _____.
   a. engineers   b. other architects   c. designers

4. A building with a steel frame does not need _____.
   a. technology
   b. thick walls
   c. stores and offices on the first floor

5. The first building with 60 floors was built only _____ years after a 50-story building.
   a. 1913   b. 4   c. 18

6. As population increases, _____ increases.
   a. immigration
   b. the number of skyscrapers
   c. the number of old buildings

7. A Chicago architect has designed a building with _____ stories.
   a. 115   b. 150   c. 210

E. Comprehension Questions

1. Why is it a surprise to find out that the first skyscraper was in Chicago?
2. Why don't buildings with steel frames need thick lower walls?
3. Name an advantage of buildings with thin lower walls.
4. Why does the text say that elevators were invented just at the right time?
5. What effect did the arrival of thousands of immigrants to the U.S. have on skyscrapers?
6. What is the tallest building in the world today?
7. What is the advantage of high-rise buildings over lower buildings?
8. Why can Japan have skyscrapers today when it couldn't before?
9. Do you think people would use 200-story buildings? What is your reason?

F. Main Idea

1. Which sentence gives the main idea in paragraph 2 (lines 6–13)?
2. Paragraph 12 (lines 85–89)?
3. Write a sentence that gives the main idea in paragraph 6 (lines 33–41).
4. Write a sentence that gives the main idea of the last paragraph.

A MISHMASH (A HODGEPODGE)

WORD STUDY

A. Word Forms
These are some common verb prefixes and suffixes.

en — encircle, enclose
-en — darken, shorten
-ize — memorize, colonize

	Verb	Noun	Adjective	Adverb
1.	compare	comparison	comparative	comparatively
2.	please	pleasure	(un)pleasant	(un)pleasantly
3.	add	addition	additional	additionally
4.	(dis)connect	connection	(dis)connected (un)connected	(dis)connectedly
5.	mix	mixture		
6.		(dis)advantage	(dis)advantageous	(dis)advantageously
7.	prevent	prevention	preventive	
8.	immigrate	immigration immigrant		
9.	popularize	popularity	popular	popularly
10.	enclose	enclosure		
11.	strengthen	strength	strong	strongly

1a. Spanish spelling is _____ easy to learn.
1b. By _____, speaking English is more difficult.
2. It was a _____ to meet you.
3. People who are afraid to fly don't like being closed in. _____, they sometimes fear heights and don't understand the technology of flying.
4a. What is the _____ between the changes in the family and woman's place in society?
4b. We had the phone _____ because we are moving tomorrow.
4c. You can't put a list of _____ sentences in one paragraph.
5. Students from several countries are _____ together in one class.
6. It is _____ to learn English. Are there any _____ to learning it?
7. _____ medicine is better than helping people after they are sick.

8. The _____ office is open from 9:00 to 5:00.

9a. _____ is very important to teenagers.

9b. Paper handkerchiefs or tissues are _____ called Kleenex. Most people call them that.

10a. The farmer put his sheep in an _____ for the night.

10b. The university admissions office included several _____ with the letter to the new student.

11a. Exercise _____ the muscles.

11b. I agree with you _____.

B. Summarizing
Write a sentence to summarize these paragraphs.

1. 1 (lines 1–5)
2. 2 (lines 6–13)
3. 4 (lines 19–25)
4. 7 (lines 42–48)
5. 8 (lines 49–56)
6. 9 (lines 57–68)
7. 10 (lines 69–75)

C. Two-Word Verbs: Review
Put the right word in the blanks.

1. There was a long line waiting to check _____ at the airport.
2. A large truck broke _____ on the highway.
3. Alice goes to the gym every weekend to work _____.
4. Do you have enough money to live _____?
5. Could you help me _____ this weekend?
6. Fixing my car turned _____ an all-day job.
7. Mr. Brown has been working too hard and has to slow _____.
8. Jean had to drop _____ of school and get a job.
9. Children don't like to put _____ their toys when they finish playing.
10. Bob was an hour late because he ran _____ _____ gas.

D. Articles

1. When people _____ think of _____ skyscrapers, they think of New York, _____ city with _____ most high-rise buildings in _____ world.

A MISHMASH (A HODGEPODGE)

2. It comes as _____ surprise to learn that Chicago, not New York, is ___ home of _____ skyscraper.
3. For centuries, _____ buildings were made of _____ stone.
4. How would _____ people get up to _____ top stories in _____ 10-story building?
5. Elisha Otis invented _____ elevator and first showed it to _____ public in 1853.
6. _____ Amazon River is in _____ tropics.
7. _____ people in my class are mostly from _____ Middle East.
8. _____ Bering Sea is in _____ North Pacific Ocean.
9. _____ Lake Superior is between _____ Canada and _____ United States.
10. _____ history of _____ England is complicated.

E. Context Clues

Many words have two meanings. What is the correct meaning in these sentences?

1. You can have **as long as** you want to do this test. There is no time limit.
   a. if   b. as much time as c. a long time

2. Mr. Rossi doesn't have enough wood to finish the table he is making. He has to buy another **board**.
   a. get on a plane b. uninteresting c. flat piece of wood

3. Maria is 10 kilos overweight so she is going to **diet**.
   a. eat less
   b. the food someone eats
   c. what a roadrunner eats

4. **Nuclear** testing is dangerous.
   a. a kind of bomb b. a kind of family c. a kind of protest

5. Greenpeace **objects** to nuclear testing.
   a. things   b. lists   c. is against

6. My brother and his wife are having family problems, but they hope they can **work** them **out**.
   a. get exercise b. work hard c. solve

LEFT-HANDEDNESS

5

Are you a leftie? If you are, you are one of millions in the world who **prefer** to use their left hand. There would be millions more left-handed people if societies didn't force them to use their
5 right hands.

    like better

    To understand left-handedness, it is necessary to look at the brain. The brain is **divided** into two hemispheres. In most right-handers, the left hemisphere is the center of language and
10 logical thinking, where they do their math problems and memorize vocabulary. The right hemisphere controls how they understand broad, general ideas, and how they respond to the five senses—sight, hearing, smell, taste, and touch.

    ÷

15   The left hemisphere of the brain controls the right side of the body, and the right hemisphere controls the left side. Both sides of the body receive the same information from the brain because both hemispheres are connected.
20 However, in right-handed people, the left hemisphere is stronger. In left-handed people, it is the right hemisphere that is stronger.

    Different handedness causes differences in people. Although the left hemisphere controls
25 language in most right-handers, 40 percent of left-handers have the language center in the right hemisphere. The other 60 percent use the left side of the brain or both sides for language.

142

Lefties not only prefer using the left hand.
30 They prefer using the left foot for kicking a ball,
because the whole body is "left-handed."

There is an increasing amount of research
on handedness. For example, one psychologist
says that left-handers are more likely to have a
35 good imagination. They also enjoy swimming
underwater more than right-handers.

Left-handedness can cause problems for
people. Some left-handed children see letters
and words backwards. They read *d* for *b* and *was*
40 for *saw*. Another problem is stuttering. Some
left-handed children start to stutter when they
are forced to write with their right hand. Queen
Elizabeth II's father, King George VI, had to
change from left- to right-handed writing when
45 he was a child, and he stuttered all his life.

Anthropologists think that the earliest people were about 50 percent right-handed and 50
percent left-handed because ancient tools from
before 8000 B.C. could be used with either hand.
50 But by 3500 B.C., the tools, which were better
designed, were for use with only one hand. More
than half of them were for right-handed people.

The first writing system, invented by the
Phoenicians (3000–2000 B.C.) in the Middle East,
55 went from right to left. The Greeks began to
write from left to right around the fifth century
B.C. because they increasingly believed that
"right" was good and "left" was bad. As time
passed, there were more and more customs con-
60 necting "left" with "bad." This belief is still
common in many countries today, and left-
handed people suffer from it.

As the centuries passed and education
spread to more levels of society, more and more
65 people became literate. As more children learned
to write, more of them were forced to write with
their right hands. In the United States, some

teachers finally started permitting schoolchildren to write with their left hands in the 1930s.
70 In parts of Europe, left-handed children were still forced to write with their right hands in the 1950s. Today in many countries, all children must write with their right hand even though they prefer using their left hand.

75 Some famous people were left-handed. Julius Caesar, Napoleon, Michelangelo and da Vinci (famous Italian artists), and Albert Einstein were left-handed. Alexander the Great (356–323 B.C.) and Queen Victoria of England were also. So
80 is Prince Charles.

Paul McCartney of the Beatles plays the guitar the opposite way from other guitarists because he is left-handed. Marilyn Monroe, the famous American movie star, was also left-
85 handed.

Are you left-handed even though you write with your right hand? Take this test to find out. Draw a circle with one hand and then with the other. If you draw them clockwise (the direction
90 the hands of a clock go in) you are probably left-handed. If you draw them counterclockwise (in the other direction), you are right-handed. The test does not always work, and some people may draw one circle in one direction and the
95 other circle in the other direction. But don't worry if you are left-handed. You are in good company.

A MISHMASH (A HODGEPODGE)

A. Vocabulary

divide	broader	backward	stutter
senses	responding	force	prefer
kick	tool		

1. The main streets of a city are _____ than the side streets. Broadway is a common street name.
2. If a left-handed person is forced to write with his right hand, he may begin to _____.
3. A car can go forward and _____.
4. Players cannot _____ the ball in basketball.
5. Would you _____ coffee or tea?
6. A blind person is lacking one of the _____.
7. Some students are shy about _____ in class.

B. Vocabulary

divided	tools	force	broad
common	counterclockwise	clockwise	permit

1. A mechanic cannot fix a car without _____.
2. Twenty _____ by four equals five (20 ÷ 4 = 5).
3. _____ means the way the hands of a clock go. _____ is the opposite.
4. Parents should not _____ their children to swim in the pool without an adult there.
5. Spiders are _____ everywhere except at the North and South Poles.
6. Governments cannot _____ people to limit the size of their family.

C. Vocabulary Review

sticks out	male	mates	nests
once in awhile	boring	suffer	crash
fear	tunnel	loss	terrified

1. A man is a _____.
2. In spring, animals search for _____.

3. Spiders and birds build _____.
4. A roadrunner's head _____ straight in front when it runs.
5. The Simplon _____ goes under the Alps between Italy and Switzerland.
6. Being afraid to fly is an illogical _____.
7. We heard a loud _____ and knew that there had been an accident.
8. Some people think baseball is _____ because it is so slow.
9. Would you be _____ to meet Frankenstein?
10. Most people only fly _____.

D. True/False/No Information

_____ 1. Some Eskimos are left-handed.
_____ 2. Most right-handers do calculus with the left hemisphere of the brain.
_____ 3. When people look at a beautiful sunset, most of them use the right hemisphere of the brain.
_____ 4. The right hemisphere controls the right side of the body.
_____ 5. Most people in the world use the left hemisphere for language.
_____ 6. Left-handedness can cause children to see letters backward.
_____ 7. It is easier to write from left to right.
_____ 8. Left-handed people are more intelligent than right-handers.

E. Comprehension Questions

1. What does the right hemisphere of the brain control?
2. Which hemisphere is stronger in left-handed people?
3. Why do lefties prefer to kick with the left foot?
4. What problems do lefties have using machines?
5. When do some left-handers start to stutter?
6. Why do anthropologists think the earliest people were equally divided between left- and right-handedness?
7. Why did the Greeks start writing from left to right?
8. What does "you are in good company" mean?
9. How can you tell if a two-year-old child is left-handed?
10. Are you left-handed?

A MISHMASH (A HODGEPODGE)

F. Main Idea

1. What sentence is the main idea for paragraph 4 (lines 23–28)?
2. Paragraph 6 (lines 32–36)?
3. Write a sentence for the main idea in paragraph 9 (lines 53–62).
4. Write the main idea of the last paragraph.

WORD STUDY

A. Word Forms

	Verb	Noun	Adjective	Adverb
1.	communicate	communication(s)	(un)communicative	
2.	exist	existence	(non)existent	
3.	prefer	preference	(un)preferential	
4.	divide	division	(in)divisible	
5.	force	force	forceful	forcefully
6.			(un)common	(un)commonly
7.	respond	response	(un)responsive	
8.	permit	permission	(im)permissible	(im)permissibly
		permit	permissive	
9.		reality	(un)real	really

1a. There have been many wonderful developments in the field of _____ in the last 20 years.

1b. I tried to get the information from the president's secretary, but she was very _____.

2. Frank told everyone he worked for a large company, but the company is _____.

3a. Professors should not give _____ treatment to the students they like.

3b. Short jackets, not long coats, are _____ by skiers.

4. Ten is not evenly _____ by three.

5a. Ms. Bush has a very _____ personality.

5b. John was _____ to leave the university because his grades were so bad.

6. It is _____ believed that sons are better than daughters.

7. The injured person _____ to the doctor's treatment. She is well now.

8a. Some psychologists say that adults should not be _____ with their children.

8b. You cannot build a house in this city without a building _____.

8c. Smoking _____ not _____ in this building.

9. It seemed _____ to Abdullah that he had finally finished his doctorate degree and was going home.

A MISHMASH (A HODGEPODGE)

B. Finding the Reason
Write the reason for each statement.

Statement	**Reason**

1. Many left-handers have to use their right hand.
2. For some people, the center of language is in the right hemisphere.
3. Both sides of the body receive the same information.
4. Lefties prefer kicking with the left foot.
5. King George VI stuttered.
6. Anthropologists think more than 50 percent of people were right-handed by 3500 B.C.
7. Paul McCartney plays the guitar differently.

C. Connecting Words
Put **after, before, when, since,** or **until** in the blanks.

1. I'll give you the book _____ I see you tomorrow.
2. People who are afraid of flying can control their fear _____ they take a class.
3. Greenpeace has been in existence _____ 1971.
4. Greenpeace was organized _____ the U.S. started nuclear testing in Alaska.
5. Sometimes _____ the roadrunner gets a piece of meat, it takes it back to its nest.
6. There were no skyscrapers _____ 1884.
7. _____ Burke started across Australia, he organized an expedition.
8. Some left-handed European children were forced to write with their right hands _____ the 1950s.

D. Missing Words
Fill in the missing words.

1. If you are, you are one _____ millions in _____ world _____ prefer _____ use their left hand.

2. _____ understand left-handedness, it is necessary _____ look _____ the brain.
3. The brain _____ divided _____ two hemispheres.
4. Both sides of _____ body receive the same information _____ the brain because both hemispheres _____ connected.
5. There is _____ increasing amount _____ research _____ handedness.
6. But _____ 3500 B.C., the tools, which _____ better designed, were for use _____ only one hand.
7. _____ the centuries passed and education spread _____ more levels _____ society, more and _____ people became _____.
8. But _____ worry _____ you are left-handed. You are _____ good company.

E. Context Clues

1. A computer is a very **complex** machine.
   a. beautiful   b. boring   c. complicated

2. Ali said he was from Palestine, but he was **actually** born in Qatar.
   a. preferably   b. maybe   c. really

3. The members of Greenpeace **discuss** a protest to get each other's ideas. Then they start planning.
   a. talk about   b. prepare   c. publish

4. Pierre has studied English for 3 months **so far**. He plans to study for 6 more.
   a. until now   b. away from home   c. altogether

5. In rain forests, dead plants **create** nutrients for living plants.
   a. take away   b. make   c. prevent

6. Most children think video games are **fascinating**. They spend hours playing them.
   a. very boring   b. very interesting   c. unpleasant

Unit

IV

SCIENCE

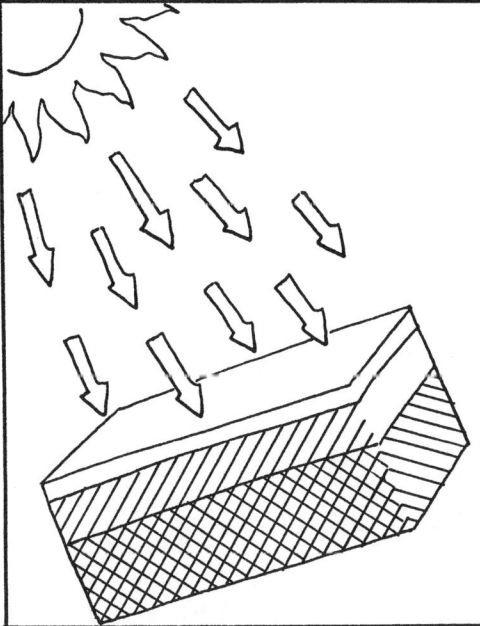

Minds are like parachutes. They only function when they are open.
—Sir James Dewar

A BIOSPHERE IN SPACE

Is it possible for people to live on another **planet** such as Mars? The Environmental Research Laboratory at the University of Arizona is designing a biosphere (*bio* means *life*, and
5 *sphere* is a circle like a ball) which could be used to colonize other planets. The author interviewed Walter Lindley, Program Coordinator at the Laboratory, about this exciting idea.

P.A.: I've been reading science fiction stories
10 about space colonies for years, but of course they were possible only in the author's imagination. Now you are **actually** preparing for a space colony. Do you really consider it possible for people to live away from the earth?

         really

15 W.L.: We believe it will be possible sometime in the future, and that's why we're working on it. But it's a very **complex** project. Our biosphere will be a complete, enclosed environment where people can be born, live their whole life, and die
20 without returning to earth. But there will have to be a perfect balance between plants, animals (including humans), and the chemical elements, that is, everything in the environment. Right now we're talking about a place for ten people to
25 live for a year. It's not like one or two men on the moon for a few weeks.

         complicated

Sun
Mercury
Venus
Earth
Mars
Jupiter
Saturn
Uranus
Neptune
Pluto

153

P.A.: What will it look like?

W.L.: We don't know yet. We call it a biosphere,
but it might not be round. It could be square or
30 any shape at all. There might be separate units
for food production. These would be connected
to the main unit. Architects and engineers are
discussing all the possibilities now. We have to
figure out what shape it should be, what mate-
35 rials to use, and how small it could be and still
support human life.

talking about

P.A.: You mentioned engineers and architects.
Who else is working on it?

W.L.: That's one of the interesting things about
40 the project. There are biologists, biochemists,
and people from different areas of agriculture.
We have specialists on almost everything in our
environment.

P.A.: It seems so unreal and impossible that it's
45 hard for me to understand it. Could you explain
a little more?

W.L.: Well, a greenhouse for growing plants in
winter is the first step toward a biosphere. This
is a closed environment except for the sun's heat
50 entering through the glass or plastic. Of course,
there is a water system from outside, and people
bring in nutrients for the plants and take out the
waste material. The biosphere will have to have
its own system to provide water that can be used
55 and reused. It will need bacteria or something
else to take care of the wastes. And it all must be
balanced perfectly, or the whole system will
break down.
     Nothing will enter the biosphere except
60 heat from the sun and information from earth.
Of course the information going in and out won't

be necessary for the biosphere to exist, but it will be very necessary for research.

The earth itself is the best example of a
65 biosphere. Nothing important enters except sunlight, and nothing leaves as waste except some heat. Everything in the earth's environment has always been balanced, except that now humans are destroying the balance more and more.

70 P.A.: Why do we want a colony on Mars? It's very exciting, but is it necessary?

W.L.: I'm sure you know that there will be a petroleum shortage in the future. Dr. Gerard K. O'Neill is a famous physicist from Princeton
75 University. He says that in 25 years we will have **satellites** in space to produce **solar** energy and send it to earth. It would be too expensive to continually send people and materials to the satellites, so the biosphere will be necessary. He
80 thinks 10,000 people could live in a space colony sometime in the future.

solar = adjective for *sun*

So far all your questions are about a space colony, but for me there's a much more interesting use of the biosphere. We can use it to do
85 all kinds of research about our own environment and how it works. By studying the biosphere, we can understand better what will happen as humans destroy tropical forests, as we **create** more carbon dioxide (CO_2) by burning fuel, and
90 as we pollute the oceans and the air. The information we get from the biosphere may keep us from destroying our own environment.

until now

make

P.A.: I agree with you that learning how to protect our own environment is the most impor-
95 tant thing we can do, both for ourselves and for our children. The world's population is increasing very fast, and we are using up our natural resources fast. We need to do everything we can

to save our environment before it's too late. I'm
100 glad you've started this **fascinating** project,   very interesting
and I hope it's successful.

A. Vocabulary

actual	planet	project	science fiction
solar	satellite	complex	carbon dioxide
unit	bacteria	consider	

1. The earth is a _____. It is part of the _____
    system.
2. _____ can cause disease. They also destroy wastes.
3. Tom said his new car cost $10,000, but the _____ figure
    was $9,980.85.
4. Julia likes to read _____.
5. The space colony might be all in one _____, or it might
    have separate ones for agriculture.
6. The government has a _____ to build a dam to store water
    for agriculture.
7. Another word for complicated is _____.
8. We must _____ both the advantages and the disadvan-
    tages before we start the project.

B. Vocabulary

create	satellite	bacteria	carbon dioxide
so far	discussed	actually	elements
balance	project	physicist	fascinating

1. CO_2 means _____.
2. Gold (Au), oxygen (O), and uranium (U) are all _____.
3. Destroying rain forests can _____ problems for the whole
    world.
4. The class _____ how to prepare for the TOEFL exam.
5. _____ there are no buildings over 110 stories high.
6. A _____ teaches or does research in physics.

7. Before the large increase in population, there was a _____ between the needs of the people and what the land could produce.
8. Much international communication is now done by _____.
9. It is a _____ experience to live in another country.

C. Vocabulary Review

energy	avoided	rush	crew
takes off	board	harmful	phobia
honestly	score	interview	initial

1. Please _____ this paper so I can show my teacher that you have read it.
2. After people _____ a plane, it _____.
3. What was the final _____ of the game?
4. Sometimes students have to _____ someone and write a composition about it.
5. Smoking is _____ to the health.
6. _____ is produced by burning fuel.
7. If you _____ through your work, you are likely to make mistakes.
8. Kumiko _____ giving a speech in class by staying home that day.
9. A road _____ is repairing the main street where I drive every day.
10. Betty said she _____ forgot to meet her friend for lunch Sunday.

D. Multiple Choice

1. Fiction is _____.
   a. true   b. imaginative   c. boring

2. The biosphere is a complicated project because _____.
   a. everything must be perfectly balanced
   b. they don't know what materials to build it from
   c. people from different professions are working on it

3. The biosphere _____ be round.
   a. must   b. will   c. might

4. The first biosphere will support _____ people.
   a. two or three   b. ten   c. ten thousand

5. A greenhouse _____.
   a. is a partly enclosed environment
   b. is a biosphere
   c. supports plant life independently

6. _____ might take care of the wastes in the biosphere.
   a. A water system
   b. Balanced nutrients
   c. Bacteria

7. Dr. O'Neill thinks _____.
   a. satellites can produce solar energy
   b. about ten people could take care of a satellite
   c. we need a space colony to study the solar system

E. Comprehension Questions

1. Why is it a complex project to create a biosphere?
2. What problems must the architects and engineers consider?
3. How is a greenhouse different from a biosphere?
4. Explain why the earth is a biosphere.
5. How does Dr. O'Neill think we will solve the energy shortage?
6. Why can we learn about our environment from the biosphere?
7. Would you like to live in a biosphere on Mars? Why or why not?

F. Main Idea

1. Write a sentence that gives the main idea for paragraph 5 (lines 28–36).
2. Paragraph 7 (lines 39–43)
3. What sentence is the main idea for paragraph 11 (lines 64–69)?
4. Write a sentence for the main idea of paragraph 13 (lines 72–81).

WORD STUDY

A. Word Forms: Verbs and Nouns
Many English words are used as both a verb and a noun. Use 10 of these examples in sentences, using some verbs and some nouns.

Verb	Noun
balance	balance
kick	kick
force	force
design	design
interview	interview
initial	initial
fear	fear
crash	crash
harm	harm
bother	bother
whistle	whistle
knock	knock

B. Noun Substitutes
What do these noun substitutes stand for? Sometimes the word isn't in the sentence before.

1. page 153, line 5 which _____
2.   line 10 they   _____
3.   linc 15 wc   _____
4.   line 16 it   _____
5. page 154, line 27 it   _____
6.   line 31 these _____
7.   line 56 it   _____
8. page 155, line 64 itself _____
9.   line 71 it   _____
10.   line 77 it   _____

C. Articles
Put an article in the blank if one is necessary.

1. _____ Environmental Research Laboratory at _____ University of Arizona is designing _____ biosphere.
2. I've been reading _____ science fiction stories about _____ space colonies for years, but of course they were possible only in _____ author's imagination.
3. Now you are actually preparing for _____ space colony.
4. We believe it will be possible sometime in _____ future.
5. But it's _____ very complex project.
6. But there will have to be _____ perfect balance between _____ plants, animals (including _____ humans), and _____ chemical elements; that is, everything in _____ environment.
7. We call it _____ biosphere.
8. These would be connected to _____ main unit.
9. Well, _____ greenhouse for growing _____ plants in winter is _____ first step toward _____ biosphere.
10. This is _____ closed environment except for _____ sun's heat entering through _____ glass or _____ plastic.

D. Cause and Effect
What is the cause of each of these effects?

Cause	Effect
1.	a. People can live their whole lives in the biosphere.
2.	b. The whole system might break down.
3.	c. The same water must be used and reused.
4.	d. We will need solar energy.
5.	e. The biosphere will be necessary to run solar energy satellites.
6.	f. We create more carbon dioxide.

E. Context Clues

1. There are two ways to plant seeds. One is to put each seed in a hole in the ground. The other is to **scatter** the seeds on the ground by the handful.
   a. spread around
   b. push into the ground
   c. plant by machine

2. When you take ice out of the freezer, it **melts**.
   a. gets colder
   b. changes to a gas
   c. changes to water

3. At night, scientists **observe** the stars, the solar system, and other objects in the sky at an observatory.
   a. write about   b. are tested on   c. look at

4. Water starts to boil at 100°C. Then it becomes **steam**.
   a. water in the form of ice
   b. very hot water
   c. water in the form of hot moisture in the air

5. A stone sinks in water. A piece of wood or paper **floats**.
   a. goes to the bottom of the water
   b. rides on top of the water
   c. gets very wet

VOLCANOES

2

Throughout history, people who lived near volcanoes made up stories to explain why they erupt. Usually they believed that the gods were showing their anger through the eruption. To-
5   day scientists can explain much about volcanoes, but they also must guess about what is happening deep inside the earth. There is still much for us to learn.

The active volcanoes of the world exist in
10 definite patterns. They are not just scattered anywhere, but are found in **chains** and groups. Three-quarters of the earth's volcanoes are in the Ring of Fire around the Pacific Ocean. There is another chain in the Atlantic, a chain in the
15 Mediterranean, and a group in Central Africa. Most of them are on coastlines or islands.

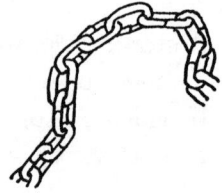

What causes volcanoes to erupt? Much of the material under the surface of the earth is melted rock called magma. Heavy layers of rock
20 push down on the magma. The magma escapes sideways or upward until it starts to push on the underside of the earth's surface. If there is a weak spot, the magma and its gases push right through the spot and explode into the air. If
25 there is a lot of gas, the eruption is violent; if there is only a little gas, the eruption is mild. The hole which forms at the top of the volcano is

called a crater. After the magma escapes to the
earth's surface, it is called lava.

30   Some volcanic eruptions are very gentle.
Kilauea, for example, on the island of Hawaii
erupts often, and tourists go to see it because the
melted rock shooting into the air is beautiful.
Scientists at the Hawaiian Volcano Observatory
35 near Kilauea have given us much knowledge
about volcanoes. Stromboli, another famous volcano, is on an island between Sicily and Italy. It
has been erupting about every half hour for 2500
years. Volcanoes like Kilauea and Stromboli
40 don't usually cause much damage.

Iceland also has nonviolent eruptions, but
they often cause damage because the hot lava
melts the snow and ice and causes floods.

Although some famous volcanoes are gen-
45 tle, most of the world's active volcanoes have
very explosive activity and violent eruptions.
The eruptions are violent because there is a long
resting period between eruptions, and a lot of
gas builds up in the magma. There have been
50 some famous eruptions from this kind of volcano.

In late 1984, strong earthquakes began
shaking the Nevado del Ruiz volcano in Colombia every day. Then it began sending out steam
55 and ash. On November 14, 1985, it erupted. A
nearby river became a sea of mud which buried
four towns. This disaster killed more than 2100
people.

Mt. Vesuvius in Italy had not erupted for a
60 thousand years, and people thought it was dead,
but in A.D. 79 it erupted and buried the city of
Pompeii in ashes. Life stopped for 2000 people
who were buried under the ashes. Today we can
visit Pompeii and see exactly what life was like
65 1900 years ago.

In 1902, Mt. Pelée on the island of Martinique in the Caribbean Sea erupted. First a huge

cloud of steam appeared at the top of the volcano. People moved into the town of St. Pierre
70 from the surrounding countryside where they
thought they would be safe because St. Pierre
was 13 kilometers from the volcano. Two weeks
later, there were several explosions that sounded
like thunder, and Mt. Pelée seemed to burst
75 apart. A huge black cloud rolled down the moun-
tainside, and in 3 minutes it covered St. Pierre.
Thirty thousand people died.

The worst eruption in history was on the
small island of Krakatoa, Indonesia, in 1883.
80 The volcano started sending out steam in the
early spring of that year, and as the weeks
passed, explosions sent out dust and ash that
killed all the plants on the island. The surface of
the sea was covered with hot, floating volcanic
85 rock.

On August 26 there was an explosion every
10 minutes, lightning appeared in the sky, and a
cloud of black steam covered the island. Then
there was a huge explosion—the loudest sound
90 ever heard by humans. The sound waves, which
broke windows 350 kilometers away, traveled
5000 kilometers. Two-thirds of the island disappeared into the crater. Water rushed in to fill the
hole, and there was a final explosion when the
95 water mixed with the magma. This caused a
huge sea wave, as tall as a 12-story building,
which rushed away from Krakatoa. The wave
covered the low islands nearby and destroyed
300 villages. Even ships in South Africa felt the
100 wave. Over 36,000 people died from the eruption
and the huge wave.

The dust from the eruption moved high
above the earth and traveled around the world at
least 12 times. For two years it formed a wall
105 between the sun and the earth, and the earth's
temperature dropped 10°C. Sometimes the sun
was green or blue. When the last of the dust fell

after several years, the island of Krakatoa had
been spread all over the earth.

110   There is no question that volcanoes are
destructive. Is there anything good about them?
People continue living near them because volcanic soil is the most productive on earth. Volcanic
areas also contain many of the world's valuable

115 metals. Many of Africa's diamonds come from
volcanic areas. Volcanoes also create geothermal
energy. *Geothermal* means *earth heat*, heat created by volcanic activity underground. This
could help solve the world's energy shortage.

120   Scientists are observing volcanoes throughout the world. They hope that by studying the
history of eruptions and the changes in a volcano
before an eruption, they will be able to tell when
one is going to happen. Humans have learned to

125 control many things about nature, but we cannot control volcanoes. However, if we can know
that an eruption is going to happen, many lives
can be saved.

A. Vocabulary

volcanoes	chain	damage	bursts
rolled	waves	patterns	melts
floods	thunder	lightning	float
valuable	erupted	definite	surface

1. When there is _____ and _____ during a
   storm, it is sometimes called an electrical storm.
2. Mt. St. Helens, a volcano in Washington State in the United States,
   _____ in 1980.
3. A gold _____ is a popular kind of jewelry.
4. There is a ring of _____ around the Pacific Ocean.
5. When a tire _____ while a car is moving, it is called a
   blowout.
6. When Peter set his pencil on the table, it _____ off onto the
   floor.

7. Huge ocean _____ hit the shore during a storm.
8. Gold and silver are _____ metals.
9. The Browns think they are going to Europe next summer, but it isn't _____.
10. Volcanoes are found in definite _____ around the world.
11. Floods cause a lot of _____ to towns and agriculture.
12. When snow _____ in the mountains, it can cause _____ _____ in the lowlands.

B. Vocabulary

surface	layer	crater	observe
geothermal	active	scattered	magma
float	damage	guess	pattern
mild	lava	ashes	steam

1. _____ energy comes from heat under the earth.
2. Melted rock inside the earth is called _____. When it leaves the _____ of the volcano, it is called _____.
3. Rocks generally sink below the _____ of the sea. However, some volcanic rock is light enough to _____.
4. The wind _____ my papers all over the room.
5. Trains used to be run by _____. Now most of them are run by electricity or diesel oil.
6. The weather has been _____ this week, even though it is winter. It hasn't been very cold.
7. Smokers put their cigarette _____ in an ashtray.
8. In a rain forest, the lower _____ of plant growth is protected by the upper layer.
9. Students who plan to become teachers usually have to _____ classes as a first step toward teaching.
10. Mr. Green is not very _____ now. He is 87 and in poor health.
11. Can you _____ what I have in this bag?

C. Vocabulary Review

For each word in the first column, find a synonym in the second column and an antonym in the third column.

		Synonyms		**Antonyms**
1.	fascinating	a. common	m.	uncomplicated
2.	complex	b. small	n.	excited
3.	so far	c. interesting	o.	forbid
4.	create	d. quiet	p.	unusual
5.	ordinary	e. complicated	q.	boring
6.	force	f. make	r.	separate
7.	broad	g. make someone do something	s.	not yet
8.	tiny	h. balance	t.	actual
9.	connect	i. consider	u.	narrow
10.	calm	j. join together	v.	unit
		k. until now	w.	destroy
		l. wide	x.	huge

D. True/False/No Information

_____ 1. Today scientists know all the details about the formation of volcanoes.

_____ 2. Inactive volcanoes exist in definite patterns.

_____ 3. More than half of the world's volcanoes are near the Pacific.

_____ 4. Most inactive volcanoes are near the sea.

_____ 5. Magma pushes through a weak spot in the earth's surface.

_____ 6. A lot of gas mixed with the magma causes a violent explosion.

_____ 7. Most of the world's active volcanoes have mild activity.

_____ 8. Krakatoa destroyed the town of St. Pierre.

_____ 9. Early people made tools from volcanic materials.

_____ 10. *Thermal* means *heat*.

E. Comprehension Questions

1. Why did people think there were gods in volcanoes?
2. Why don't scientists understand everything about the activity below the surface of the earth?

3. Why is the *Ring of Fire* a good name?
4. Why are some eruptions more violent than others?
5. Why do Iceland's nonviolent volcanoes cause damage?
6. Why can some volcanic rock float?
7. What caused the huge sea wave after Krakatoa erupted?
8. How did Krakatoa become spread all over the world?
9. What are some advantages of volcanoes?

F. Main Idea
Write or copy a sentence that is the main idea for these paragraphs.

1. 2 (lines 9–16)
2. 6 (lines 44–51)
3. 7 (lines 52–58)
4. 13 (lines 110–119)

WORD STUDY

A. Word Forms

Verb	Noun	Adjective	Adverb
1. discuss	discussion		
2. consider	consideration	(in)considerate	(in)considerately
3.	complexity	complex	
4. fascinate	fascination	fascinating	fascinatingly
		fascinated	
5. create	creation	(un)creative	creatively
	creativity		
6. value	value	valuable	
7. observe	observation	(un)observant	
	observatory		
8. act	action	(in)active	actively
	activity		
9. explain	explanation	(un)explainable	
10. believe	belief	(un)believable	(un)believably

1. After a long _____, the architects decided to change the design.
2. Marge is a very _____ person. She thinks of others and what they want, instead of thinking of herself most of the time.
3. The _____ of modern society affects family patterns.
4. Mark is going to study geology because he is _____ by rocks.
5. Pablo Picasso was a very _____ artist. He was known for his _____.
6. Most people want to have friends. They _____ the friendship of people they like.
7. When the director of the English program _____ classes, she writes up an _____ report.
8. Pierre has become _____ in the stamp club because he is too busy to attend. Stamp collecting used to be his favorite _____.
9. Can scientists give a clear _____ of what actually happens deep in the earth? No, some of the details are _____ so far.
10. Scientists consider it _____ that gods create volcanic eruptions.

B. Sequencing
Put these sentences about Krakatoa in the right order. Number 1 is done for you.

_____ a. The dust traveled around the world.
_____ b. Water rushed in to fill the hole.
___1___ c. The volcano started sending out steam.
_____ d. The water mixed with magma.
_____ e. All the plants on the island died.
_____ f. There was a huge explosion.
_____ g. A huge sea wave was created.
_____ h. Lightning appeared.
_____ i. Two-thirds of the island disappeared into the crater.
_____ j. There was a final explosion.

C. Two-Word Verbs
Numbers 2 and 3 have the same expression twice.

mix up   — mistake one thing for another
dress up   — put on special clothes
have on   — be wearing
look out   — be careful
spread out — spread over a certain area or time

1. Don't try to learn 40 irregular verbs in one day. _____
   them _____ over a week or two.
2. People usually _____ for a party. Children like to _____
   in their parents' old clothes and play that they are adults.
3. First she _____ her homework assignments and gave the
   reading homework to the wrong teacher. Then she found out she had done
   the wrong page. She was _____.
4. _____ ! There's a child in the street!
5. Mike _____ his running clothes because he just came back
   from jogging.

D. Prepositions and Two-Word Verbs

1. _____ history, people who lived _____ volcanoes made _____ stories to explain why they erupt.
2. Scientists must guess what is happening deep _____ the earth.
3. The active volcanoes _____ the world exist _____ definite patterns.
4. Most of them are _____ coastlines or islands.
5. Heavy layers _____ rock push _____ _____ the magma.
6. If there is a weak spot, the magma and its gases push right _____ the spot and explode _____ the air.
7. The hole that forms _____ the top _____ the volcano is called a crater.
8. The eruptions are violent because there is a long resting period _____ eruptions, and a lot _____ gas builds _____ _____ the magma.
9. Mt. Vesuvius _____ Italy had not erupted _____ a thousand years.
10. _____ 1902, Mt. Pelée _____ the island _____ Martinique _____ the Caribbean Sea erupted.
11. Krakatoa started sending _____ steam _____ early spring.

E. Context Clues

1. When a violent volcanic eruption **occurs**, there is usually damage.
   a. damages   b. scatters   c. happens

2. We could not breathe without the earth's **atmosphere**.
   a. the air around the earth
   b. the movement of the earth around the sun
   c. the water on the surface of the earth

3. When Carol is doing research, she often finds useful information in several places in the same book. She puts a **strip** of paper in each place so she can find it again easily.
   a. a large white paper to take notes on
   b. a long, thin piece of paper
   c. a round piece of paper

4. Wheat, corn, cotton, and fruit are valuable farm **crops**.
   a. plants people eat
   b. food that grows on low plants
   c. plants farmers grow

5. One cold January day in Montreal, dark clouds appeared in the sky, the day grew colder, and millions of **snowflakes** began to fall.
   a. pieces of ice   b. rain   c. pieces of snow

SNOW AND HAIL

3

Millions of people in the world have never seen snow. Others see more of it than they want to. Hail is much commoner; it **occurs** even in deserts.

<small>5</small> Each tiny piece of snow is called a snowflake, and each flake has six sides or six points. Billions of snowflakes fall every winter, and the amazing fact is that each one is different. A snowflake is as individual as someone's hand-<small>10</small> writing or **fingerprint**.

A snowflake forms inside a winter storm cloud when a **microscopic** piece of dust is **trapped** inside a tiny drop of water. This happens in the **atmosphere** 10 kilometers above <small>15</small> the earth. The water freezes around the dust, and as this flake is blown by the wind, it collects more drops of water. These drops freeze too, and the snowflake becomes heavy enough to start falling to earth. As it falls, it passes through <small>20</small> areas where the temperature and humidity vary. It collects more and more tiny drops of water, and the shape continually changes. Some drops fall off and start to form new snowflakes.

This sounds simple, but it is actually very <small>25</small> complex. It is so complex that mathematicians using computers are just beginning to understand what happens. Every change in temperature and humidity in the air around the

happens

can't escape
air around the earth

173

snowflake causes a change in the speed and
30 pattern of the snowflake's formation as it makes
its trip to the earth. Since no two flakes follow
exactly the same path to the ground, no two
snowflakes are exactly alike. However, they are
all six-sided. So far, no one understands why this
35 is **so**.   true

Hail is a small round ball of alternating
layers of snow and clear ice. It forms inside
thunderclouds. There are two theories about
how hailstones form.

40 One theory says that hail forms when drops
of water freeze in the upper air. As they fall, they
collect more drops of water, just as snowflakes
do. They also collect snow. The ice and snow
build up in layers. If you cut a hailstone, you can
45 see these alternating layers.

The other theory says that hail starts as a
raindrop. The wind carries it higher into the
atmosphere where it gets covered by snow. It
becomes heavy and begins to fall. As it falls, it
50 gets a new layer of water which freezes. Then
the wind carries it back up to the snow region,
and it gets another layer of snow. This can happen several times. Finally the hailstone is too
heavy to travel on the wind, and it falls to the
55 ground.

Only thunderstorms can produce hail, but
very few of them do. Perhaps only one in 400
thunderstorms create hailstones.

Hail usually falls in a strip from 10 to 20
60 kilometers wide and more than 40 kilometers
long.

A hailstone is usually less than 8 centimeters in **diameter**. However, hailstones can be
much bigger than that. Sometimes they are as
65 big as baseballs. The largest ever recorded
weighed over 680 grams and had a diameter of
13 centimeters.

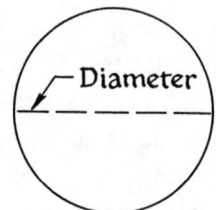

Diameter

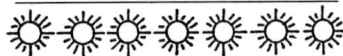

Hail can do a lot of damage to agriculture, especially since hail usually appears in midsummer, when the plants are partly grown. If the crops are destroyed, it is too late to plant more and the farmer has lost everything. The most damage is done by hailstones that are only the size of peas. In one terrible hailstorm in 1923 in Rostov in the USSR, 23 people and many cattle were killed.

Snow can cause damage too. It can cave in the roof of a building. A heavy snowstorm can delay airplane flights and cause automobile accidents. Farm animals sometimes die in snowstorms, and when country roads are closed by the snow, people can be trapped in their cars and freeze to death. Yet there is nothing more beautiful than the sight of millions of snowflakes falling on a still, moonlit night. That is when people think of the beauty, and not the science, of snowflakes.

A. Vocabulary

fact	exactly	midsummer	traps
so	records	snowflake	microscopic
alternating	strip	points	fingerprint

1. Hail falls in a _____ about 40 kilometers long.
2. Volcanoes occur in patterns. This is a _____.
3. The weather is warm or hot in _____.
4. Trappers set _____ to catch animals.
5. Some people still believe that volcanic eruptions are caused by angry gods, but we know this isn't _____.
6. Every _____ has six sides or six _____.
7. The boys and girls lined up in _____ rows.
8. Bacteria are _____. They can't be seen without a microscope.
9. The government _____ the daily amount of rainfall.

B. Vocabulary

occur	fingerprint	fact	atmosphere
theory	hail	so	crop
trap	microscope	diameter	exactly

1. No two individuals are _____ the same, not even twins.
2. When did the last eruption of Kilauea _____?
3. The police _____ criminals.
4. The distance across a circle is called the _____.
5. Humans are polluting the earth's _____.
6. Albert Einstein developed a very important _____ about relativity.
7. Cacao (chocolate) is an important _____ in West Africa.
8. _____ can destroy a farmer's crops.

C. Vocabulary Review
Match the words with their definition.

1. hire _____
2. compare _____
3. in addition _____
4. immigrant _____
5. earthquake _____
6. story _____
7. prefer _____
8. divide _____
9. respond _____
10. permit _____
11. discuss _____
12. carbon dioxide _____
13. solar _____
14. create _____

a. movement of the earth
b. look for similarities
c. $\div$
d. pleasant
e. give a job to
f. CO_2
g. floor
h. frame
i. of the sun
j. talk about
k. person who goes to live in another country for the rest of his or her life
l. answer
m. like better
n. allow
o. and
p. make

D. Short Answers
Write **hail**, **snow**, or **hail and snow** after each of these sentences.

1. As it is blown by the wind, it collects water.
2. It occurs only in the colder regions of the world.
3. It is formed of layers of ice and snow.
4. It can destroy crops.
5. It can cause the death of humans.
6. It is sometimes formed around a piece of dust.
7. It always has six sides or six points.
8. It is produced only by thunderstorms.
9. It is a small round ball.
10. It can cause damage.

E. Comprehension Questions

1. Why do all snowflakes have six sides or six points?
2. Snowflakes start forming around two things. What are they?
3. What does a change in humidity do to the formation of a snowflake?
4. Why are no two snowflakes alike?
5. Where do hailstones form?
6. What causes both snowflakes and hail to fall to the ground?
7. About how big is the average hailstone?
8. How does hail destroy crops?
9. Give an example of how snow can be destructive.
10. Which is more destructive, hail or snow? Why?
11. Do roadrunners ever see hail?

F. Main Idea

1. Write a sentence for the main idea of paragraph 2 (lines 5–10).
2. Paragraph 4 (lines 24–35)
3. Which sentence is the main idea of paragraph 11 (lines 68–76)?

WORD STUDY

A. Word Forms: Negative Prefixes

These are common negative prefixes. Put a word from number 1 in the first sentence and so on. Use the right form of the word.

1. **dis-**   dislike, discomfort, displease, disconnect, dishonest
2. **un-**   uncreative, unprepared, unobservant
3. **non-**   nonsmoking, nonalcoholic, nonviolent, nonindustrial
4. **in-**   inactive, inconsiderate, incorrect, inexpensive
5. **im-**   impossible, improbable, immovable, imperfect
6. **il-**   illogical, illiterate
7. **ir-**   irregular, irreligious
8. **mis-**   misbehave, misspell, misunderstand, misspeak

1. Alice always _____ the television during a thunderstorm.
2. Bering and his men were _____ for living on the island after their boat sank.
3. Coke and Pepsi are _____ drinks.
4. It is _____ to eat something in front of someone else and not offer them some.
5. It is _____ that women will have equal rights with men in this century.
6. It is _____ to think that someone who is _____ is unintelligent.
7. _____ verbs must be memorized.
8. There are three _____ words in your homework paper.

B. Summarizing

Write a summary of the information about snow. Write five or six sentences.

C. Compound Words
Make compound words using a word from the first column and one from the second.

1. take _____   a. by
2. blow _____   b. water
3. thunder _____   c. storm
4. in _____   d. walk
5. under _____   e. off
6. under _____   f. lands
7. through _____   g. ground
8. near _____   h. side
9. side _____   i. out
10. low _____   j. out

D. Articles

1. _____ snowflake forms inside _____ winter storm cloud when _____ microscopic piece of dust is trapped inside _____ tiny drop of _____ water.
2. This happens in _____ atmosphere 10 kilometers above _____ earth.
3. _____ water freezes around _____ dust, and as this flake is blown by _____ wind, it collects more drops of _____ water.
4. As it falls, it passes through _____ areas where _____ temperature and _____ humidity vary.
5. It is so complex that _____ mathematicians using _____ computers are just beginning to understand what happens.
6. Every change in _____ temperature and _____ humidity in _____ air causes _____ change in _____ speed and _____ pattern of snowflake's formation as it makes its trip to _____ earth.
7. _____ hail is _____ small round ball of _____ alternating layers of _____ snow and _____ clear ice.

E. Context Clues

1. The energy from the sun is **inexhaustible**.
   a. very tired   b. can never be used up c. never gets tired

2. Glass and water are **transparent**. Iron and wood are not.
   a. expensive   b. can float   c. can be seen through

3. The Rio Grande River forms part of the **boundary** between Mexico and the United States.
   a. border   b. pattern   c. highway system

4. When Masako visited England, she had to **convert** her Japanese money into pounds.
   a. change   b. buy   c. earn

5. Brazil **exports** coffee to Europe. Japan **exports** cars to China.
   a. sells to another country
   b. produces
   c. trades

PHOTOVOLTAIC CELLS — ENERGY SOURCE OF THE FUTURE

4

As population increases and countries industrialize, the world's demand for energy increases. Our supply of petroleum and gas is limited, but the photovoltaic cell offers a solution
5 to the problem of a future energy shortage. This cell can become an important source of energy. In fact, it seems almost like magic. The photovoltaic cell changes sunlight directly into energy, and energy from the sun is clean, easily avail-
10 able, **inexhaustible**, and free, with the right   can't be used up
equipment.

Did you ever reach to open the door at a store or hotel and see it open by itself? Does your camera always let in the right amount of light
15 for your pictures? These are two examples of uses of photovoltaic cells. They are also used in calculators and watches, remote telecommunication units, and in central power stations to produce electricity. Another important use is in the
20 space exploration program. This program could not exist without the energy produced by photovoltaic cells.

The photovoltaic cell is simple. It has a **transparent** metallic film at the top. Below this   can be seen through
25 is a layer of silicon (Si). A metal base is at the bottom.

The sunlight falls on the boundary between the two different types of semiconductors in the

photovoltaic cell, the silicon and the metal base.
30 A conductor is something that electricity can
pass through. Water and metals conduct electricity, but wood does not. A semiconductor conducts electricity poorly at low temperatures, but
when heat or light is added, conductivity is in-
35 creased.

As the light falls on this boundary between
the two types of semiconductors, it creates an
electric current. The sunlight is **converted** di-   changed
rectly into electricity.

40   Another advantage is that this cell is solid-
state; that is, there are no moving parts. **Since**   because
there are no moving parts to break down, the cell
will last a long time if it is protected from damage.
However, this protection is important. If the top
45 of the cell even gets dusty, less light enters, and
the cell doesn't work as efficiently as it should.

In addition, silicon is one of the commonest
elements in the world; for example, sand is made
up mostly of silicon. However, the chemical
50 preparation of the silicon for use in a photovoltaic cell was very expensive at first. Now the cost
has decreased. Scientists hope that in the future
they will be able to produce it in long sheets the
way plastic for plastic bags is made today.

55   About 18 percent of the sunlight that
reaches the cell is converted into electricity. This
is a small amount, so many cells must be used to
create a reasonable amount of electricity. However, technology can be developed to make the
60 cells more efficient and raise this to 27 percent.

What does this mean to the world? Photovoltaic cells have several advantages over fossil
fuels (petroleum, oil, and coal). Fossil fuels that
we use today were formed from plants and ani-
65 mals that lived millions of years ago. Those
plants and animals were able to exist because of   can be seen or
the sun. **Obviously**, we can't wait a million   understood easily

SCIENCE

years for more fossil fuels. The photovoltaic cell
70 gives us the ability to produce energy directly
from the sun. The sun's energy can be converted
for our use immediately.

At the present time, gas and oil are expen-
sive. Developing countries cannot **export**   sell to other countries
75 enough agricultural products and other raw ma-
terials to import the fuel that they need to produce energy. At the same time, petroleum supplies are limited, and in a few decades they will
run out. However, the supply of sunlight is lim-
80 itless, and most of the poor countries of the
world are in the tropics where there is plenty of
sunlight.

The photovoltaic cell has another very important advantage. It is a clean source of energy.
85 The fossil fuels that we use today are the main
source of the pollution in our atmosphere.

It took only a decade for scientists to know
that solar energy from photovoltaic cells was not
just a dream. They have already proven that it
90 can become an important source of energy. By
the end of the century, it will be cheaper to
produce electricity with solar cells than from
petroleum. The photovoltaic cell can be the solution to one of the most serious problems in the
world today.

A. Vocabulary

photovoltaic cell	inexhaustible	silicon	semiconductors
solid-state	fossil	import	exports
magic	raw material	reasonable	source

1. Scientists think that the _____ will be an important en-
    ergy source for the future.
2. The number of snowflakes is limitless and _____.
3. A photovoltaic cell has two different types of _____.
4. Petroleum is a _____ fuel.

5. The _____ of a river is the place it begins.
6. Children like to see _____ shows.
7. Japan _____ television but has to _____ oil.
8. _____ (Si) is used to make glass.
9. Iron is the main _____ for making steel.

B. Vocabulary

demanded	current	since	efficient
obvious	last	reasonable	transparent
boundary	fossil	conducts	converts

1. Electric _____ can pass through metal because metal _____ electricity.
2. The factory workers _____ higher pay for their work.
3. Much of the _____ between Canada and the United States is a straight line.
4. Abdullah missed the test _____ he was late for class.
5. Thirty minutes is a _____ length of time for a short test.
6. It is _____ that Carlos copied Maria's homework. The papers are exactly alike.
7. It is more _____ for 30 people to ride in a bus than in 30 different cars.
8. Glass is _____.
9. A hydroelectric power station _____ water power into electricity.

C. Vocabulary Review
Underline the word that does not belong with the others.

1. hail, snowflake, trap, rain
2. steam, crater, lava, ash
3. create, damage, destroy, harm
4. definite, sure, exact, chain
5. satellite, planet, star, sun
6. consider, object, discuss, talk over

7. backward, forward, clockwise, sideward
8. physicist, anthropologist, chemist, geologist
9. burst, eruption, flood, earthquake
10. fly, bee, ant, snake

D. Multiple Choice

1. Solar energy will not be _____ in the future.
   a. expensive   b. easily available   c. limitless

2. Sunlight first enters a photovoltaic cell through _____.
   a. a metal base   b. a metallic film   c. a layer of silicon

3. The place where the two semiconductors meet is called the _____.
   a. border   b. conductor   c. boundary

4. A semiconductor works best _____.
   a. when there is wood available
   b. when the temperature is low
   c. when light or heat is added

5. A photovoltaic cell _____ light into an electricity.
   a. currents   b. converts   c. conducts

6. The cell must be protected from _____.
   a. dust   b. light   c. movement

7. At first, these cells were expensive to make because _____.
   a. the chemical preparation of silicon was expensive
   b. silicon is expensive and hard to find
   c. it is hard to keep dirt off the cells

8. Most of today's air pollution comes from _____.
   a. automobiles
   b. burning fossil fuels
   c. factories

E. Comprehension Questions

1. Why do we need a new way to produce energy?
2. Describe a photovoltaic cell.
3. Give three advantages of photovoltaic cells over fossil fuels.
4. In what part of the cell is the electric current created?
5. What does *solid-state* mean?
6. What happens when a photovoltaic cell gets dusty?
7. Why was energy from photovoltaic cells expensive in the beginning?
8. How can these cells help third world countries?
9. Why are photovoltaic cells so important in the space program?

F. Main Idea

1. Which sentence is the main idea of paragraph 1 (lines 1–11)?
2. Paragraph 9 (lines 61–71)?
3. Write a sentence for the main idea of paragraph 2 (lines 12–22).
4. Write the main idea of paragraph 6 (lines 40–46).

WORD STUDY

A. Word Forms

This is a common use of an adjective. There are two sentence patterns.

It is + adjective _____.

It is necessary to memorize irregular verbs.
It is beautiful to walk by the ocean on a moonlit night.

It is important that you fill out these papers immediately.
It is wonderful that you took first place in the competition.

	Verb	Noun	Adjective	Adverb
1.	trap	trap		
		trapper		
2.	alternate	alternate	alternate	alternately
		alternative	alternative	alternatively
3.	occur	occurrence		
4.	bound	boundary	bound	
5.	theorize	theory	theoretical	theoretically
6.		efficiency	(in)efficient	(in)efficiently
7.		reasonableness	(un)reasonable	reasonably
8.	exhaust	exhaustion	(in)exhaustible	(in)exhaustibly
9.		transparency	transparent	transparently
10.	convert	conversion		

1. When an animal is _____, it can't get away.
2a. There is no _____ to our plan. We can find no _____ plan.
2b. The government can give poor people free food or _____, it can give them money to buy food.
3. There were three _____ of a breakdown in the nuclear power plant.
4. Norway is _____ by Sweden, Finland, the Soviet Union, the Atlantic Ocean, and the North Sea.
5a. Scientists _____ about the center of the earth, but they can't know for sure.

5b. _____, there are black holes in space.

5c. It is still _____ that the brain works because of electrical connections.

6. It is _____ to write by hand instead of using a typewriter.

7. It is _____ to expect a student to memorize 50 new words a day.

8. Scott and his men became _____ on their journey back from the South Pole.

9. _____ is a characteristic of water and glass.

10. Missionaries try to _____ people to their religion.

B. Finding the Reason
Write the reason for each statement.

Statement	Reason
1. An entrance door at a hotel opens by itself.	
2. Electricity can pass through water.	
3. The first photovoltaic cells were very expensive.	
4. These cells can help the Third World.	
5. Energy from the sun is inexhaustible.	
6. The photovoltaic cell can't break down.	
7. The photovoltaic cell might work inefficiently.	

C. Two-Word Verbs

get in   —arrive; for example, gets in a bus or plane
bring up —raise children
show up —appear
stand by —wait for a seat on an airplane without a ticket
leave out—skip, forget to include something

1. When Ali did his homework, he _____ the third exercise. He forgot to do it.

2. What time does the train from Paris _____?

3. The airline said there were no seats available on this flight, but if someone doesn't _____, I can have that seat. I have to _____ until everyone has boarded. Sometimes standby seats are cheaper, but you take the chance of not getting on the flight.

4. Mary was born on a farm, but she was _____ in a small town.

D. Missing Words
Fill in the blanks with any word that fits in the sentence.

1. _____ population increases and countries industrialize, _____ world's demand _____ energy increases.
2. This cell _____ become _____ important source _____ energy.
3. _____ you ever reach _____ open _____ door _____ a store _____ hotel _____ see it open _____ itself?
4. The space program could _____ exist _____ the energy produced _____ photovoltaic cells.
5. It has _____ transparent metallic film _____ the top. Below this is _____ layer of silicon (Si).
6. The sunlight falls _____ the boundary _____ the two different types _____ semiconductors, _____ silicon _____ the metal base.
7. This cell _____ solid-state; _____ is, _____ are no moving parts.
8. Since there _____ no moving parts to break _____, the cell _____ last _____ long time _____ it is protected _____ damage.
9. If _____ top of _____ cell even _____ dusty, less _____ enters, _____ the cell _____ work as efficiently _____ it should.

E. Context Clues

1. France, England, the United States, Japan, South Africa, and Australia are examples of countries in the two **temperate** zones.
   a. the hot, humid tropics
   b. near the North or South Poles
   c. between the tropics and the Arctic or Antarctic Circle

2. At **dawn** the sky begins to get light and the sun appears.
   a. sunrise
   b. sunset
   c. a storm with thunder and lightning

3. Millions of monarch butterflies **migrate** every fall from North America to southern Mexico and Central America. In the spring they return to the north.
   a. travel a long distance because of the season
   b. travel a long distance to lay eggs
   c. return to their home

4. Every night Mohammed sets his **alarm** clock. In the morning it wakes him up.
   a. a clock that makes a noise at a certain hour
   b. a clock that tells the day, month, and year
   c. a clock that is in the bedroom

5. The private school organized several **events** for Parents' Day. There were races for the small children, a soccer game, a musical program, a picnic, and meetings with the teachers.
   a. any kind of game or sport
   b. anything that happens
   c. programs for children

BIOLOGICAL CLOCKS

5

If you have ever flown across several time zones, you have experienced jet lag. You arrived in a new time zone, but your body was still living on the time in the old zone. You were wide awake
5 and ready for dinner in the middle of the night, and you wanted to sleep all day.

People suffer from jet lag because all living things have a biological clock. Plants and animals are all in rhythm with the natural divisions
10 of time — day and night and the seasons.

At sunrise, plants open their leaves and begin producing food. At night, they rest. In the temperate zones of the earth, trees lose their leaves in fall as the days grow shorter, and there
15 is less sunlight. In the spring, leaves and flowers begin growing again as the days lengthen.

Rain sets the rhythm of desert plants. Plants in the desert may appear dead for months or even years, but when it begins to rain, the
20 plants seem to come to life overnight. The leaves turn green, and flowers appear. The plants produce seeds quickly, before the rain stops. These seeds may lie on the ground for years before the rain starts the cycle of growth again. The plants'
25 biological clock gave the signal for these things to happen.

At **dawn** most birds wake up and start   sunrise
singing. When the sun goes down, they go to

191

sleep. When spring arrives, they start looking for
30 a mate. When winter comes, some birds migrate
to a region with a warmer climate. Their biological clock tells them it is time to do all these
things.

Animals that live near the sea and depend
35 on both the land and water for their food have
their biological clocks set with the tides. When
the tide goes out, they know it is time to search
for the food that the sea left behind it.

Some insects seem to set their alarm clock
40 to wake up at night. They are out all night
looking for food and then sleep during the day.
Honeybees have a very strong sense of time.
They can tell by the position of the sun exactly
when their favorite flowers open.

45 Some French scientists did an experiment
with honeybees. They put out sugar water every
morning at 10:00 and at noon, and the bees came
to drink the water at exactly the right time.
Then the scientists put the sugar water in a
50 room that was brightly lit 24 hours a day. They
started putting the sugar water out at 8:00 p.m.
It took the bees a week to find it at the different
hour, but from then on they came to eat in the
evening instead of in the morning.

55 Later the scientists took the honeybees to
New York. The bees came for the food at the
time their bodies told them, only it was 3:00 p.m.
New York time. Their bodies were still on Paris
time.

60 Humans, like other animals, have a biological clock that tells us when to sleep and eat. It
causes other changes too. Blood pressure is
lower at night, the heartbeat is slower, and the
body temperature is a little lower. We even go
65 through several levels of sleep, cycles of deep and
light sleep.

Other **events** occur in cycles too. More babies are born between midnight and dawn than

anything that happens

at any other time. More natural deaths occur at
70 night, but more heart attacks happen early in
the morning. Most deaths from diseases in hospitals occur between midnight and 6 a.m. Some
police say there are more violent crimes and
traffic accidents when there is a full moon.
75   The honeybees in the experiment reset
their biological clock for different feeding hours.
Humans do this too. People who work at night
learn to sleep during the day and eat at night.
Students who fly halfway across the world to
80 study in another country get used to the new
time zone after a few days. When they go home,
they change back again. Our bodies are controlled by a biological clock, but we can learn to
reset it at a different time.

85

How to **Lessen** Jet Lag
make less, decrease

1. Try not to become exhausted before
you leave. Get plenty of sleep and leave
enough time to get to the airport and check in
without having to hurry.
90   2. Wear **loose** clothing, and take your
shoes off while you are in your seat.
loose ≠ tight

3. Walk around the plane and move
around in your seat.

4. Figure out breakfast time in the time
95 zone you are flying to. Four days before your
flight, start a feast (eating a lot) and fast
(eating nothing or very little) schedule. On the
fourth day before you fly, eat three heavy
meals. If you drink coffee, tea, or cola drinks
100 that contain caffeine, have them only between
3:00 and 5:00 p.m. On the third day before
your flight, eat very lightly—salads, light
soups, fruits, and juices. Again, have drinks
with caffeine only between 3:00 and 5:00 p.m.
105 On the next to the last day before you leave,
feast again. On the day before you leave, fast.
If you are flying west, drink caffeinated drinks

110
in the morning; if you are going east, drink them between 6:00 and 11:00 p.m.

5. On the day you leave, have your first meal at the time people in the new time zone eat breakfast. If it is a long flight, sleep on the plane until the new breakfast time, and don't drink any alcohol. When you wake up, have a

115
big meal. Stay awake and active, and eat at the new time zone hours.

A. Vocabulary

signal	position	pressure	attack
alarm	experiments	event	jet lag
temperate	migrate	heartbeat	fast

1. Countries with _____ climates have four different seasons.
2. A photovoltaic cell has to be in the right _____ for the sunlight to enter.
3. A wedding is an important _____ in anyone's life.
4. Students usually have to do _____ in chemistry class.
5. Some people _____ for religious reasons.
6. When the fire _____ sounded, everyone left the building.
7. Doctors listen to a person's _____ through a stethoscope to see if there are any irregularities.
8. High blood _____ can cause a serious illness.
9. Pilots don't usually suffer from _____ because they never stay in the new time zone very long.

B. Vocabulary

rhythm	dawn	temperate	tides
feast	lessens	migrate	signal
pressure	caffeine	loose	experience

1. Chocolate, tea, coffee, and cola drinks contain _____.
2. The police officer gave a _____ for the cars to stop.

3. Some birds _____ to a warmer climate in the winter.
4. The villagers prepared a _____ to entertain the visiting government officials.
5. There are high and low _____ in the ocean twice a day.
6. The sun rises at _____.
7. Rock music has a very strong _____.
8. _____ is the opposite of *tight*.
9. Aspirin _____ the effects of a headache.

C. Vocabulary Review

stroke	stand for	tools	senses
units	project	rolls	waves
guess	valuable	mild	surface

1. USSR _____ the Union of Soviet Socialist Republics.
2. A carpenter cannot work without _____.
3. Water, light, and sound travel in _____.
4. You can often use the context to _____ what a word means.
5. Dust on the _____ of a photovoltaic cell makes it work inefficiently.
6. Hearing is one of the five _____.
7. A ball or other round object _____.
8. This textbook has five _____.
9. The biosphere is a special _____ at the Environmental Research Laboratory.
10. Diamonds are _____.

D. True/False

_____ 1. *Jet lag* means your body is in one time zone but your biological clock is in another.

_____ 2. Plants begin producing nutrients when the sun rises.

_____ 3. Plants in Iceland and Greenland can produce nutrients 24 hours a day during the summer.

_____ 4. A biological clock gives birds the signal that it is time to migrate.

_____ 5. Animals that live near the sea search for food at night when it is safer.

_____ 6. The honeybees in the experiment reset their biological clock.

_____ 7. After a few days, the bees probably changed their biological clock to New York time.

_____ 8. The human biological clock affects many parts of the body.

_____ 9. Humans cannot change their biological clock once it is set, but bees can.

_____ 10. You can decrease the effects of jet lag.

E. Comprehension Questions

1. What makes desert plants produce seeds?
2. Why do birds wake at dawn?
3. How do honeybees know when a flower opens?
4. Why do they want to know when a flower opens?
5. What is the time difference between New York and Paris?
6. Why should you wear loose clothing on a long flight?
7. Why should you have breakfast at breakfast time in the new time zone on the day you leave?

F. Main Idea
Copy or write a sentence for the main idea of these paragraphs.

1. 4 (lines 17–26)
2. 9 (lines 55–59)
3. 10 (lines 60–66)
4. 12 (lines 75–84)

WORD STUDY

A. Word Forms: Adjectives

Both the -**ing** form of the verb (the present participle) and the -**ed** form (the past participle) are used as adjectives. The -**ed** form often shows that the noun received the action, or it describes how a person feels. The -**ing** form often shows some action that the noun took, or it describes an object or possibly a person. However, there are many exceptions.

> David was **bored** because the movie was **boring**.
> Tom is **interested** in stamps. He thinks stamps are **interesting**.
> Mary is an **interesting** person because she can talk about a lot of different things.

Put the right form of each verb in the sentence.

1. (exhaust) Climbing a mountain is _____ work.
2. (exhaust) Al was _____ after the soccer game.
3. (demand) Mr. Davis is a very _____ teacher. He makes the students work hard and do their best.
4. (alternate) There are two kinds of electric current, direct and _____.
5. (trap) The _____ animal couldn't escape.
6. (damage) A _____ car needs to be fixed.
7. (guess) Children like to play _____ games.
8. (fascinate) Monopoly is a _____ game for some people.
9. (complicate) American football is a _____ game.
10. (terrify) Being in an airplane crash is a _____ experience.

B. Connecting Words
Connect a sentence from the first column with one from the second column using **since**, **when**, **until**, or **even though**.

1. Magma is pressed down by heavier rock.
2. It has been snowing.
3. Chris stopped drinking coffee in the evening.
4. Birds start singing.
5. A photovoltaic cell is efficient.
6. The bees were ready to eat.

a. It finds a weak place to escape.
b. It was only 3:00 p.m. in New York.
c. It kept her awake.
d. It becomes dusty.
e. The sun went down.
f. The sun rises.

C. Sequence
Put these sentences about the French experiment in the right order.

_____ a. The scientists took the bees to New York.
_____ b. Some French scientists did an experiment.
_____ c. They put the sugar water out at 8:00 p.m.
_____ d. They put the sugar water out at 10:00 a.m. and noon.
_____ e. The bees looked for food at 3:00 p.m. New York time.
_____ f. The bees took a week to find the food at a different time.
_____ g. The bees came every evening at 8:00 p.m.

D. Prepositions

1. If you have ever flown _____ several time zones, you have experienced jet lag.
2. You arrived _____ a new time zone, but your body was still living ____ the old zone.
3. You were wide awake and ready _____ dinner _____ the middle ____ the night.
4. Plants and animals are all _____ rhythm _____ the natural divisions _____ time.
5. _____ the temperate zones _____ the earth, trees lose their leaves _____ fall as the days grow shorter.

6. Plants _____ the desert may appear dead _____ months or even years.
7. Some animals depend _____ the sea for their food.
8. Some insects wake _____ _____ night.
9. Honeybees can tell _____ the position _____ the sun exactly when their favorite flowers open.
10. They put _____ sugar water every morning _____ 10:00 and noon.

E. Word Forms: Semi- and Hemi-

Hemi- is a prefix that means **half. Hemisphere** is the most common word with this prefix.

Semi- is a prefix that means **half** or **partly**. These are some common words with this prefix:

semiconductor
semicolon (;)
semitransparent
semisolid (Toothpaste, ice cream, and asphalt are all semisolid.)
semifinal (in sports competitions)
semifinalist
semitropical (Hawaii is semitropical, but it is not in the tropics.)
semiweekly (twice a week; some meetings are held semiweekly and some
        magazines are published semiweekly)
semimonthly (twice a month)
semiyearly (twice a year)
semiprivate (a hospital room with two or three patients)
semisweet (Some chocolate is semisweet.)

Use six of these words in interesting sentences.

F. Context Clues

1. After Isamu got hit in the nose with a baseball, his nose started to **swell**.
   a. get bigger   b. smell   c. alarm

2. Old Mr. Rossi's **vision** is getting bad, so he wears strong glasses.
   a. health   b. ability to see   c. blood pressure

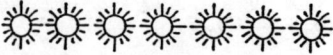

3. Doctors do not know how to **cure** the common cold.
    a. make better   b. do research on   c. protect

4. Maria's hair hangs down into her eyes. She keeps pushing it back off her **forehead**.
    a. the top part of the face
    b. the top of the head
    c. the part of the face under the eyes

5. There are five **patients** waiting to see the doctor.
    a. people who are very calm
    b. people who have a medical problem
    c. people who are studying medicine

Unit V

MEDICINE AND HEALTH

Early to bed and early to rise makes a man healthy, wealthy, and wise.
                                                              —Benjamin Franklin

HEADACHES

Some little man is inside your head, pounding your brain with a **hammer**. Beside him, a rock musician is playing a **drum**. Your head feels as if it is going to explode. You have a
5   headache and you think it will never go away.

Doctors say there are several kinds of headaches. Each kind begins in a different place and needs a different treatment.

One kind starts in the arteries in the head.
10   The arteries **swell** and send pain signals to the   get larger
brain. Some of these headaches start with a
change in **vision**. The person sees wavy lines,   ability to see, sight
black dots, or bright spots in front of the eyes.
This is a warning that a headache is coming. The
15   headache occurs on only one side of the head.
The vision is blurred and the person may vomit
from the pain. These headaches, which are called
migraine headaches, are more frequent in
women than in men. Sleep is the best cure for
20   them.

Cluster headaches, which also start in the
arteries, are called cluster headaches because
they come in clusters or groups for two or three
months. Then there are no more for several
25   months or even years. A cluster headache lasts
up to two hours and then goes away. At the
beginning of the headache, the eyes are red and
watery. There is a **steady** pain in the head.   continuing

🧍🧍🧍🧍🧍🧍🧍🧍

When the pain finally goes away, the head is
30 **sore**. Men have more cluster headaches than
women do.

painful

    The muscle headache, which starts in the
muscles in the neck or **forehead**, is caused by
tension. A person works too hard, is nervous
35 about something, or has problems at work, at
school, or at home. The neck and head muscles
become tense, and the headache starts. A muscle
headache usually starts in the morning and gets
worse as the hours pass. There is a steady pain,
40 pressure, and a bursting feeling. Usually aspirin
doesn't help a muscle headache very much.

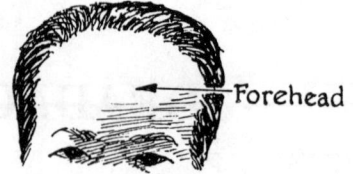

—Forehead

    About 40 percent of all headaches start in
the head and neck muscles. Another 40 percent
start in the arteries.

45   How do doctors treat headaches? If a person
has frequent headaches, the doctor first has to
decide what kind they are. Medicine can help,
but there are other ways to treat them.

    The doctor asks the patient to analyze his
50 or her daily living patterns. A change in diet or
an increase in exercise might stop the headaches. If the patient realizes that difficulties at
home, at work, or at school are causing the
tension, it might be possible to make changes
55 and decrease these problems. Psychological
problems and even medicine for another
physical problem can cause headaches. The
doctor has to discuss and analyze all these patterns of the patient's life. A headache can also be
60 a signal of a more serious problem.

of the body

    Everyone has headaches from time to time.
If they continue over several days, or keep
recurring, it is time to talk to a doctor. There is
no magic cure for headaches, but a doctor can
65 help control most of them because of recent
research.

occurring again

MEDICINE AND HEALTH

A. Vocabulary

pounded	swells	blur	migraine
clusters	sore	forehead	aspirin
recur	drums	pain	hammer
artery	nervous	vomit	cures

1. _____ means to *happen again*.
2. If your arm is _____, it hurts. You have a _____ in your arm.
3. The _____ is the top part of the face.
4. People all over the world use _____ to make music.
5. _____ helps some kinds of headaches.
6. When we went to our friend's apartment, we knocked and then _____ on the door, but no one answered.
7. One kind of headache is called a _____.
8. A _____ is one kind of tool.
9. When you put air in a bicycle tire, the tire _____ until it fits the wheel exactly.
10. After the TOEFL test, the students gathered in small _____ to talk about it.
11. Do you feel _____ when you have to take a test?

B. Vocabulary

ache	warned	blurred	arteries
vision	hammer	drum	forehead
vomit	cures	physical	swell
steady	patients	muscles	tense

1. When you are sick and in pain, your stomach may protest and make you _____.
2. The teacher _____ the children that they had to behave or there would be no party.
3. People in the hospital are called _____.
4. While Pat was swimming she got water in her eyes. Everything looked _____.
5. Students feel _____ before an important exam.

6. Tension in the _____ of the neck can cause a headache.
7. The farmers were happy when a _____ rain continued all night.
8. _____ carry blood from the heart to the rest of the body.
9. Today there are _____ for many diseases that used to kill people.
10. People with poor _____ wear glasses or contact lenses.
11. You may get a <u>stomach</u> _____ if you eat too much.
12. A complete _____ examination is necessary for anyone entering the army.

C. Vocabulary Review: Antonyms
Match the opposites.

1. fiction _____
2. scatter _____
3. active _____
4. fact _____
5. obvious _____
6. last _____
7. export _____
8. loose _____
9. fast _____
10. lessen _____

a. point
b. import
c. nonfiction
d. unclear
e. microscope
f. run out
g. gather
h. increase
i. inactive
j. theory
k. feast
l. tight

D. Multiple Choice

1. When someone sees black dots or wavy lines, this is a change in _____.
   a. blurring   b. clusters   c. vision

2. A migraine headache causes _____.
   a. blurred vision   b. red and watery eyes   c. a bursting feeling

3. _____ is the best cure for migraines.
   a. Sleep   b. Aspirin   c. Arteries

4. _____ have more of the kind of headache that leaves the head sore.
   a. Women   b. Men   c. Older people

5. A _____ headache usually starts in the morning and gets worse.
   a. migraine   b. cluster   c. muscle

6. Tension causes a _____ headache.
   a. migraine   b. cluster   c. muscle

7. The muscle and the _____ headache are the most common.
   a. migraine   b. cluster   c. warning

8. Medicine is _____ headaches.
   a. the best treatment for
   b. not usually helpful for
   c. one way to treat

9. A change in a patient's life patterns can _____.
   a. help cure headaches   b. cause headaches   c. both a and b.

E. Comprehension Questions

1. Describe a migraine headache.
2. Describe a cluster headache.
3. Describe a muscle headache.
4. Which kind of headache affects more women than men?
5. What are some things that can cause a muscle headache?
6. If you have a headache, will aspirin help?
7. Why does a doctor analyze the life patterns of a headache patient?

F. Main Idea
Write the main idea of these paragraphs.

1. 2 (lines 6–8)
2. 3 (lines 9–20)
3. 8 (lines 49–60)

WORD STUDY

A. Word Forms

	Verb	Noun	Adjective	Adverb
1.	press	pressure		
2.	experiment	experiment	experimental	experimentally
3.	migrate	migration		
4.	lessen	least	less	
5.	warn	warning		
6.	pain	pain	painful	painfully
			painless	painlessly
7.	swell	swelling	swollen	
8.	recur	recurrence		
9.	tense	tension	tense	tensely
10.	prove	proof	proven	

1. The _____ of heavy rocks on magma causes the magma to escape from a weak place in the earth's surface.
2. The first tests of a nuclear bomb were _____.
3. Scientists study the _____ of birds.
4. The pain of some headaches _____ by aspirin.
5a. A fire alarm is a _____ to leave the building.
5b. A red light _____ people there is danger.
6. A broken arm is _____.
7. Dan hurt his hand and now it is _____.
8. After the fifth _____ of a bad headache, Mark went to a doctor.
9. _____ causes muscle headaches.
10. Scientists have definite _____ that photovoltaic cells convert sunlight directly into energy. This _____ some years ago.

B. Scanning

Scan the text to put these sentences in the right column. Write both the letter of the sentence below and the number of the line in the text where you find the idea.

Migraine   **Cluster**   **Muscle**

a. They come in groups.
b. It starts in the neck or forehead.
c. It is caused by tension.
d. There is a change in vision.
e. There may not be any for several years.
f. Aspirin doesn't help.
g. Sleep helps.
h. It occurs on only one side of the head.
i. It lasts for two hours or less.
j. Problems at work can cause it.

C. Noun Substitutes

What do these words stand for?

1. page 203 line 2 him   _____
2.   line 4 it   _____
3.   line 14 This   _____
4.   line 20 them   _____
5.   line 21 which   _____
6. page 204 line 32 which   _____
7.   line 49 his or her _____
8.   line 65 them   _____

D. Articles

1. Beside him, _____ rock musician is playing _____ drum.
2. Each kind begins in _____ different place and needs _____ different treatment.
3. One kind starts in _____ arteries in _____ head.
4. _____ arteries swell and send _____ pain signals to _____ head.
5. Some of these headaches start with a change in _____ vision.

6. _____ person sees _____ wavy lines, _____ black dots, or _____ bright spots in front of _____ eyes.
7. This is a warning that _____ headache is coming.
8. _____ headache occurs on only one side of _____ head.
9. _____ vision is blurred and _____ person may vomit from _____ pain.
10. _____ sleep is _____ best cure for them.

E. Verb + Adjective

These verbs are usually followed by an adjective: **be, feel, become, seem, act, appear, look, smell, taste**.

She is sick.   He appears tired.
She feels sick.   He looks tired.
She became sick a week ago.   It smells good.
He seems tired.   It tastes good.
He acts tired.

Use each verb in an interesting sentence.

F. Context Clues

1. Saudi Arabia has **a great deal of** petroleum.
   a. some   b. a lot of   c. too much

2. **At times** you can feel a rock musician pounding a drum in your head.
   a. sometimes   b. at a certain hour   c. always

3. Tom always **confuses** Japanese people with Chinese since their physical appearance can be similar.
   a. signals   b. mixes up   c. introduces

4. Billy is five years old. Sometimes he wakes up in the middle of the night and cries. He has **nightmares**.
   a. bad dreams   b. drums   c. alarm clocks

5. Love, hate, and anger are **intense** feelings.
   a. strong   b. opposite   c. mild

6. Children from ages thirteen to nineteen are **adolescents**.
   a. young   b. teenagers   c. adults

7. Mary has a bad **habit** of playing with her hair all the time.
   a. something that bothers her
   b. morning activity
   c. something she does often

2

SLEEP AND DREAMS

"Oh sleep! it is a gentle thing,
Beloved from pole to pole."

Samuel Taylor Coleridge, a famous British
poet, wrote these words over a hundred years
5 ago. Most people would agree with him. Sleep is
very important to humans; the average person
spends 220,000 hours of a lifetime sleeping. Until about thirty years ago, no one knew much
about sleep. Then doctors and scientists began
10 doing research in sleep laboratories. They have
learned **a great deal** by studying people as they   a lot
sleep, but there is still much that they don't
understand.

Scientists study the body characteristics
15 that change during sleep, such as body temper-
ature, brain waves, blood pressure, **breathing**,   taking air in and out of
and heartbeat. They also study rapid eye move-   the body
ment (REM). These scientists have learned that
there is a kind of sleep with REM and another
20 kind with no rapid eye movement (NREM).

NREM is divided into three stages. In stage
one, when you start to go to sleep, you have a
pleasant floating feeling. A sudden noise can
wake you up. In stage two, you are sleeping more
25 deeply, and a noise will probably not wake you. In
stage three, which you reach in less than 30
minutes, the brain waves are less active and

stretched out. Then, within another half hour, you reach REM sleep. This stage might last an
30 hour and a half and is the time when you dream. For the rest of the night, REM and NREM alternate.

Body movement during sleep occurs just before the REM stage. The average person
35 moves about 30 times during sleep each night.

Sleep is a biological need, but your brain never really sleeps. It is never actually blank. The things that were on your mind during the day are still there at night. They appear as
40 dreams, which people have been discussing for centuries. **At times** people believed that dreams had magical powers or that they could tell the future.

    sometimes

Sometimes dreams are terrifying, but they
45 are usually a collection of scattered, **confused** thoughts. If you dream about something that is worrying you, you may wake up exhausted, sweating, and with a rapid heartbeat. It is possible that dreams have a **positive** effect on our
50 lives. It may be that during a dream the brain can concentrate on a problem and look for different solutions.

    mixed up

    positive ≠ negative

Researchers say that normal people may have four or five REM **periods** of dreaming a
55 night. The first one may begin only a half hour after falling asleep. Each period of dreaming is a little longer, the last one lasting up to an hour. Dreams also become more intense as the night continues. **Nightmares** usually occur toward
60 dawn.

    lengths of time

    bad dreams

People dream in color, but many don't remember the colors. Certain people control some of their dreams. They make sure they have a happy ending.

65 Many people talk in their sleep, but it is usually just confused half sentences. They might feel embarrassed when someone tells them they

were talking in their sleep, but they probably didn't give away any secrets.

70 Sleepwalking is most common among children. They usually grow out of it when they are **adolescents**. Children don't remember that they were walking in their sleep, and they don't usually wake up if the parent leads them back to
75 bed.

teenagers

Some people have the habit of grinding their teeth while they sleep. They may wake up with a sore jaw or a headache, and they can also damage their teeth. Researchers don't know why
80 people talk, walk, or grind their teeth while they are asleep.

There are lots of jokes about snoring, but it isn't really funny. People snore because they have trouble breathing while they are asleep.
85 Some snorers have a condition called sleep apnea. They stop breathing up to 30 or 40 times an hour because the throat muscles relax too much and block the airway. Then they breathe in some air and start snoring. This is a danger-
90 ous condition because if the brain is without oxygen for 4 minutes, there will be **permanent** brain damage. Sleep apnea can also cause irregular heartbeats, a general lack of energy, and high blood pressure.

always, forever

95 Most people need from 7½ to 8½ hours of sleep a night, but this varies with individuals. Babies sleep 18 hours, and old people need less sleep than younger people. If someone continually sleeps longer than normal for no **apparent**
100 reason, there may be something physically or psychologically wrong.

adjective for *appear*

You cannot save hours of sleep the way you save money in the bank. If you have only 5 hours of sleep for three nights, you don't need to sleep
105 an extra 9 hours on the weekend. And it doesn't do any good to sleep extra hours ahead of time when you know you will have to stay up late.

What should you do if you have trouble sleeping? Lots of people take sleeping pills, but
110 these are dangerous because they are habit-forming. If you take them for several weeks, it is hard to stop taking them.

Doctors say the best thing is to try to relax and to avoid bad habits. If you always go to bed
115 and get up at about the same time, this sets a rhythm in your life. Caffeine keeps people awake, so don't drink caffeine drinks in the evening. Smoking and alcohol can also keep you awake. You may have trouble sleeping if you
120 have a heavy meal just before you go to bed. Eat earlier in the evening.

You may also have trouble sleeping if you have a problem or something else on your mind. This is when you need to relax. As you lie in bed,
125 tense the muscles in your feet and then relax them. Continue up the body, tensing and relax-ing the muscles until you reach the head. Start with the feet again if you are still tense. Then remember some pleasant experience you had
130 and relive it. If you are thinking about a problem or about something exciting that is going to happen the next day, get up and write about it. That will help take it off your mind. You can also get up and read or watch television. Be sure to
135 choose a book or show that is not too exciting, or you may get so interested that you won't want to go to sleep even when you feel sleepy.

Sleep is important to humans. We spend a third of our lives sleeping, so we need to under-
140 stand everything we can about sleep.

Sleep well! Sweet dreams!

♀♀♀♀♀♀♀♀♀

A. Vocabulary

stage	periods	normal	habit
oxygen	embarrassed	confused	positive
a great deal	at times	sweat	concentrate
nightmare	grinds	snore	block

1. It is hard to _____ on your homework if your roommate is playing loud music.
2. It is not _____ to have a headache for a week. You should go to a doctor.
3. In _____ one of a volcanic eruption, the volcano sends out smoke.
4. A _____ is a bad dream.
5. _____, a headache begins without warning.
6. The school day is divided into several _____, one for each class.
7. Marcel _____ coffee with a coffee grinder.
8. Sylvia has a _____ of having a cup of coffee as soon as she gets home from work.
9. Hard exercise makes you _____.
10. A Mercedes-Benz car costs _____ of money.
11. Do you _____ when you sleep?
12. There is no reason to feel _____ when you make a mistake in class.

B. Vocabulary

confused	positive	intense	adolescents
jaws	apnea	apparently	sweat
habit	block	permanently	breathe

1. Fish can _____ underwater; people cannot.
2. The _____ summer heat of the Arabian Desert can be very dangerous if you're not careful.
3. *Negative* is the opposite of _____.
4. David was _____ about the date, so he missed the meeting.
5. Someone with sleep _____ stops breathing many times during the night.

6. An immigrant plans to stay in a new country _____.
7. The professor seems to be very busy. _____ he has a lot of work to do.
8. _____ are not children, but they are not grown up either.
9. The teeth are in the upper and lower _____.
10. A car accident can _____ a highway.

C. Vocabulary Review
Match the words with the definitions.

1. melt _____   a. middle
2. mid- _____   b. distance across a circle
3. strip _____   c. fingerprint
4. crops _____   d. reasonable
5. diameter _____   e. no moving parts
6. inexhaustible _____ f. change from a solid to a liquid
7. solid-state _____   g. can be seen through
8. source _____   h. because
9. transparent _____   i. long, thin piece
10. boundary _____   j. place
11. since _____   k. happening
12. position _____   l. can't be used up
13. event _____   m. place something comes from
                                          n. border
                                          o. any plants a farmer grows

D. True/False

_____ 1. We spend about a third of our lives sleeping.
_____ 2. Researchers now understand nearly everything about sleep.
_____ 3. NREM sleep comes before the REM stage.
_____ 4. After the three stages of NREM, REM lasts the rest of the night.
_____ 5. Dreams occur during the REM stage, but the brain is normally blank the rest of the time.
_____ 6. A dream about an unhappy event can change your heartbeat.
_____ 7. Nightmares occur early when dreams are short.
_____ 8. People dream in color.

_____ 9. Sleep apnea is the cause of some snoring.

_____ 10. It is a good idea to sleep a few extra hours on the weekend if you know you have a lot of work to do the next week.

_____ 11. Five or six hours of sleep is enough for some people.

_____ 12. The best thing to do when you have trouble sleeping is to take sleeping pills.

E. Comprehension Questions

1. How have researchers learned about sleep?
2. What does REM mean?
3. At what stage of sleep do people move around?
4. How do dreams change as the sleep period continues?
5. Why do people feel embarrassed if they talk in their sleep?
6. Can sleepwalking be dangerous? Give a reason for your answer.
7. Why do some people grind their teeth while they sleep?
8. How can sleep apnea cause brain damage?
9. Name three things that can keep you awake.
10. How does a problem keep you from sleeping?

F. Main Idea
Find or write a sentence for the main idea of these paragraphs.

1. 3 (lines 22–32)
2. 5 (lines 36–43)
3. 7 (lines 53–60)
4. 13 (lines 95–101)

MEDICINE AND HEALTH

WORD STUDY

A. Word Forms

	Verb	Noun	Adjective	Adverb
1.		(ab)normality normalcy	(ab)normal	(ab)normally
2.		habit	habitual	habitually
3.	concentrate	concentration		
4.	confuse	confusion	confused	
5.		intensity	intense	intensely
6.		adolescence	adolescent	
7.	breathe	breath breathing	breathless	breathlessly
8.		permanence	permanent	permanently
9.	loosen	looseness	loose	loosely
10.	(dis)appear	(dis)appearance	apparent	apparently

1a. _____, classes begin at 8, but there is a special meeting today.

1b. Sleep apnea is an _____.

2. The present tense is used for _____ actions.

3a. Great _____ is necessary for the game of chess.

3b. Most of Australia's population is _____ on the east coast.

4. There was a lot of _____ about the new class schedule, but now it is all cleared up and things are going smoothly. At first, the students were _____.

5. Susan feels everything very _____.

6. _____ is a difficult time for young Americans and their parents.

7. Tom spoke _____ because he was so excited.

8. Nora married a German and is going to live _____ in Germany.

9. Carol _____ her belt because it was too tight.

10. The plane got in an hour ago, but Mohammed hasn't called. _____ he wasn't on it.

B. Scanning
Write short answers and the line number from the text for these questions.

1. In what stage of NREM can a sudden noise wake you up?
2. Why do people snore?
3. Why is it a bad idea to take sleeping pills?
4. How many REM periods of dreaming do normal people have?
5. What did some people use to believe about dreams?
6. What should you do if you can't sleep because you are thinking about an exciting event the next day?
7. Is it possible to control dreams?
8. Can you save up on sleep ahead of time?
9. How many times a night does an average person move?
10. How many hours a day do babies sleep?

C. Connecting Words
Connect a sentence from the first column with one in the second using these words: **before**, **after**, **although**, and **since**.

1. People move in their sleep.
2. Scientists don't know everything about sleep.
3. We shouldn't laugh about snoring.
4. Don't eat a heavy meal.
5. Go to bed and get up at about the same time.
6. The REM stage begins.

a. You go to bed.
b. It isn't really funny.
c. The REM stage begins.
d. This sets a rhythm in your life.
e. They have learned a lot in the last 30 years.
f. The NREM stage begins.

D. Missing Words
Write any word that is correct for the blanks.

1. Sleep is very important _____ humans; _____ average person spends 220,000 hours of _____ lifetime sleeping.
2. Then doctors _____ scientists began doing research _____ sleep laboratories.
3. They have learned _____ great deal _____ studying people as they slept.

4. Scientists study _____ body characteristics that change _____ sleep.
5. NREM _____ divided _____ three stages.
6. You reach stage three _____ less _____ 30 minutes.
7. Sleep is _____ biological need, _____ your brain never really sleeps.
8. _____ things that were _____ your mind during _____ day are still there _____ night.
9. _____ times people believed _____ dreams had magical powers _____ that they could tell _____ future.
10. _____ is possible _____ dreams have _____ positive effect _____ our lives.

E. Context Clues

1. When you have a cold, you feel **miserable**.
   a. very unhappy   b. very reasonable   c. very steady

2. Today there are **remedies** for diseases that people used to die from.
   a. medicines   b. cures   c. aspirin

3. The teacher was busy, so Katsuko **volunteered** to help the new student with her schedule.
   a. did it without being asked
   b. waited for the teacher to choose someone
   c. avoided

4. What is the **worth** of learning Japanese if you are never going to Japan?
   a. occurrence   b. value   c. pain

5. Mr. Thomas sat reading the paper. **Meanwhile**, his two children were doing their homework.
   a. unpleasant   b. although   c. at the same time

THE COMMON COLD

3

Your head aches and you sneeze and cough. Your nose is all stuffed up, and it keeps running, so you have to blow it every few minutes. You know by these symptoms that you have a cold, and you feel completely **miserable**. You're not sure if you will live through the day.

Everyone suffers from the common cold at some time or other. It isn't a serious illness, but over a billion dollars a year is spent on different kinds of cold medicine every year. This medicine can relieve the symptoms. That is, it can make you cough less, make your headache less intense, and stop your nose running for a while. However, it can't cure your cold. So far, there is no cure for the common cold and no medicine to prevent it.

Even though there is no cure or preventive medicine for colds, people have all kinds of ideas about how to prevent and treat colds. Some people think that if you eat lots of onions, you won't catch cold. Others say that you should avoid getting wet and **chilled** or you will catch cold. However, this is apparently not so. In an experiment in England, a group of volunteers took a bath, put on cold wet clothing, and stood in cold rooms. Others stood outside in a cold rain until they were wet through to the skin. The

very unhappy

cold

researchers didn't find any connection between
30 being wet and chilly and catching a cold.

Dr. Linus Pauling, winner of the 1954
Nobel prize for chemistry, did experiments with
vitamin C. He says his experiments prove that if
you take 1 to 2 grams a day of vitamin C, it will
35 prevent colds. Other researchers have tested this
theory for years. They have not been able to find
that large amounts of vitamin C have any effect
on colds. **Meanwhile**, millions of dollars are   at the same time
spent on vitamin C every year. This money is
40 possibly all wasted.

Colds are caused by a virus. Viruses are
even smaller than bacteria, and they cause different kinds of diseases. So far, scientists have
found over 200 kinds of viruses that cause colds.
45 Some diseases can be prevented by a vaccine.
This liquid is **injected** into the arm and the
person is safe from catching that disease. However, it is probably impossible to develop a vaccine that could work against 200 different vi-
50 ruses. Certainly no one would want to have 200
different shots, one for each cold virus, even if
they were available.

One problem with the common cold is that
the symptoms are very similar to the symptoms
55 of influenza, or flu for short. Influenza is a much
more serious disease, especially for **pregnant**
women, people over 65, and people already suf-
fering from another disease, such as a heart
problem. Even doctors cannot always tell the
60 difference between the symptoms without doing
laboratory tests. One difference between colds
and flu is fever. A person with a cold does not
have a high body temperature, but about half of
all flu patients do.

65 A similarity between colds and flu is that
they are both contagious. One person catches a
cold or the flu from another person; they don't
begin inside the body as heart disease does.

Researchers continue searching for a way to cure or prevent colds. Since colds and flu are closely related diseases, scientists hope that if
70 they find a cure for one, it will also have an effect on the other.

Doctors don't know what causes colds, but they are beginning to learn how they spread. When scientists discovered in the 1950s that
75 viruses cause colds, it seemed logical to believe that they were spread when people sneezed and coughed. They believed that the explosive cough or sneeze sent the viruses shooting out into the air and then entering the mouth or nose of
80 anyone nearby.

However, research shows that this is not true. Most cold viruses are spread through the hands. When you have a cold and blow your nose, you get viruses on your hands. Then you
85 touch another person's hand, and when that person touches his or her mouth, nose, or eyes, the virus enters the body. It isn't even necessary to touch the person directly. Cold viruses spread when roommates or members of a family touch
90 the same dishes, towels, and furniture. You can even pick up a virus when you touch the **doorknob** on your classroom door, or when you touch things in public buildings.

It seems completely illogical, but kissing
95 apparently doesn't spread colds. In one study, volunteers with a cold kissed volunteers without a cold. Only 8 percent without a cold caught one.

How can you use all this information for your own good health? Students are in close
100 contact in the classroom, the cafeteria or dining room, and dormitories or apartments. When someone you know catches a cold, try to avoid physical contact with that person. If you catch a cold yourself, keep your towel and dishes sepa-
105 rate from everyone else's. Try not to touch things that belong to others. Don't touch other

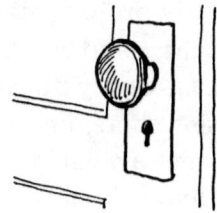

people, and don't shake hands. Explain why, however; you don't want people to think you are
110 impolite. Wash your hands often if you have a cold or if anyone around you has one.

Colds are miserable. It is worth the trouble to try to avoid catching them or giving them to others.

A. Vocabulary

cough	prizes	polite	stuffed
meanwhile	contagious	sneeze	miserable
chilled	vitamin	vaccines	influenza

1. _____ is more serious than a cold.
2. When you have a cold, you _____ and _____.
3. A pillow is _____ with feathers, cotton, or polyester.
4. Some people like to have their fruit _____ instead of at room temperature.
5. Sweden gives Nobel _____ every year to people who have created great things.
6. When you have a headache, you probably feel _____.
7. Babies should receive _____ to prevent common childhood diseases. Then they won't catch these _____ diseases.
8. Roald Amundsen reached the South Pole and began the journey back to his ship. _____, Captain Scott and his men were trapped in their tent by blizzards.
9. In most countries, it is _____ to shake hands when you meet someone.

B. Vocabulary

fever	contact	vitamins	symptoms
relieve	volunteer	viruses	injected
pregnant	worth	contagious	doorknob

1. You have to turn the _____ to open a door.
2. When your temperature is above normal, you have a _____.

3. There is no physical _____ in tennis. The players don't touch each other while they play.
4. Ms. Davis is _____. She is going to have a baby in May.
5. How much is gold _____ today?
6. Colds are caused by _____.
7. A vaccine is usually _____ into the arm.
8. Aspirin can _____ some headaches.
9. What are the _____ of a cold? How do you know you have one?
10. Thousands of people _____ to work for the Red Cross without pay.

C. Vocabulary Review

raw materials	attacked	dawn	tide
hammer	drummer	record	pounded
swell	arteries	forehead	recurring

1. Blood is carried from the heart through the _____.
2. If you hit your thumb with a _____, the thumb will probably _____ up.
3. Sometimes the sky is beautiful at _____.
4. Tom got hit in the _____ with the ball.
5. The army _____ at dawn to surprise the enemy.
6. Rita has a _____ pain in the stomach. It comes and goes.
7. The waves move higher up on the beach as the _____ comes in.
8. Iron and cotton are _____.
9. Dan _____ on the table to get everyone's attention.
10. Every rock music band has a _____.
11. The government keeps a _____ of the birth of every child.

D. Multiple Choice

1. Coughing and sneezing are _____ of a cold.
   a. miserable   b. stuffs   c. symptoms

2. Cold medicine _____ cold.
   a. can cure
   b. can relieve the symptoms of
   c. can prevent

3. An experiment in England showed that _____.
   a. getting chilled probably causes colds
   b. keeping warm and dry probably prevents colds
   c. getting chilled probably doesn't cause a cold

4. Which one of these sentences is not true?
   a. Researchers have shown that vitamin C can prevent colds.
   b. Dr. Linus Pauling's research shows that vitamin C prevents colds.
   c. People take vitamin C because they believe it prevents colds.

5. _____ prevent colds.
   a. There is no vaccine to
   b. There will probably be a vaccine in the future to
   c. You can have a vaccine injected into your arm to

6. Most colds spread _____.
   a. by hand contact
   b. when people cough and sneeze
   c. through kissing

7. The best way to avoid getting colds is to _____.
   a. avoid touching people who have colds or the objects they use
   b. avoid getting chilled or wet
   c. avoid standing near people who have a cold

E. Comprehension Questions

1. Name the symptoms of a cold.
2. What does cold medicine do for a cold?
3. Is it worth the expense to take vitamin C?
4. Why isn't it likely that someone will develop a cold vaccine?
5. How do colds spread?

6. Do you think you should or should not shake hands with someone who has a cold? Why?
7. Why can't a doctor tell if a person has a cold or the flu?

F. Main Idea

What is the main idea of these paragraphs?

1. 2 (lines 7–16)
2. 4 (lines 30–39)
3. 5 (lines 40–51)
4. 6 (lines 52–63)

WORD STUDY

A. Word Forms

	Verb	Noun	Adjective	Adverb
1.		(im)politeness	(im)polite	(im)politely
2.	stuff	stuff		
		stuffing		
3.	relieve	relief	relieved	
4.	volunteer	volunteer	(in)voluntary	(in)voluntarily
5.	inject	injection		
6.		pregnancy	pregnant	
7.		contagion	contagious	contagiously
8.	lengthen	length	long	
9.	reason	reason	(un)reasonable	(un)reasonably

1. The idea of _____ is different from one country to another.
2a. A pillow got torn, and the _____ started coming out.
2b. Most pillows are _____ with feathers or polyester.
3. Mary felt _____ when she found out her daughter had arrived safely at her grandparents' place.
4. Mark did not go into the army _____. He went because it is the law that all young men must serve in the army.
5. Children don't like to have _____.
6. A human _____ lasts 9 months.
7. Heart trouble is not _____.
8. In spring, the days start to _____.
9. Mehdi was very angry. We tried to _____ with him, but he was completely _____ and wouldn't listen at all.

B. Cause and Effect
Write the effect for each of these causes.

Cause   **Effect**

1. A cold virus enters the body.
2. People take cold medicine.
3. People take vitamin C.
4. A vaccine is injected into the body.
5. A person with a cold touches a doorknob.

C. Two-Word Verbs

grow out of — A child stops doing or feeling something as she or he grows older.
get out of   — avoid doing
show up   — appear, arrive
put off   — delay
read up on — get facts and information on a subject by reading

1. Hiroko always tries to _____ talking in front of the class because she doesn't like to do it.
2. Tom had planned to go to the shopping center today, but he _____ it _____ until the weekend because he's so busy.
3. Children _____ sleepwalking when they become adolescents.
4. Marge is going to _____ photovoltaic cells because she wants to know more about them.
5. Bob didn't _____ for the party until almost midnight.

D. Articles

1. Everyone suffers from _____ common cold at some time or other.
2. It isn't _____ serious illness, but over _____ billion dollars _____ year is spent on _____ cold medicine.
3. _____ people have all kinds of _____ ideas about how to cure and prevent _____ colds.
4. In _____ experiment in _____ England, _____ group of _____ volunteers took _____ bath, put on _____ cold wet clothing, and stood in _____ cold rooms.

5. _____ others stood outside in _____ cold rain until they were wet through to _____ skin.
6. _____ researchers didn't find any connection between being wet and chilly and catching _____ cold.
7. Dr. Linus Pauling, _____ winner of _____ 1954 Nobel prize for _____ chemistry, did _____ experiments with _____ vitamin C.

E. Context Clues

1. Adults should never **strike** children, even when the children misbehave.
   a. hit   b. help   c. block

2. Alice couldn't swim very well, but she swam way out into the middle of a lake. She was too tired to swim back to shore, and her head kept going under the water. Finally, she **drowned**.
   a. rested   b. died in the water   c. concentrated

3. How do you think your parents will **react** when you tell them you are going to marry someone from another country?
   a. act in response to a situation
   b. start doing some activity
   c. act again

4. Paul has a new car and **so do I**.
   a. I am too.   b. I do too.   c. I think it is true.

5. A photovoltaic cell cannot **function** efficiently if it has dust on it.
   a. breathe   b. confuse   c. work

6. Take this umbrella with you **in case** you need it.
   a. if maybe   b. such as   c. at times

CPR

CPR stands for cardiopulmonary resuscitation. *Cardio* is a medical word for *heart*. *Pulmonary* is a medical word for **lungs**. *Resuscitate* means to *bring back to life*. CPR starts
5 someone's lungs and **heart** functioning again after they have stopped.

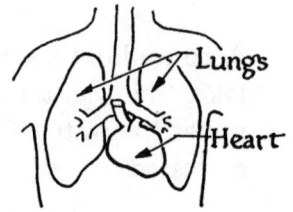

It is an amazing idea that there is a cure for sudden death. It is equally amazing that this magic is not done by today's high technology.
10 Any ordinary person can do it. You use your own lungs to breathe into the patient's mouth and start his or her lungs working. You push on the heart with your hands to make it start beating again. It is as easy as that.

15 The heart is a large muscle that pumps blood through the arteries. It is located in the center of the **chest** behind the **breastbone**. The lungs are at either side of the heart. Air enters the nose and mouth and moves through
20 the airway to the lungs, bringing oxygen into the body. As the blood moves through the lungs, it picks up the oxygen and carries it to the cells throughout the body. At the same time that the blood picks up the oxygen, it leaves carbon diox-
25 ide as a waste material, and the lungs breathe it out through the airway.

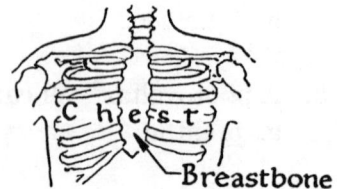

When the heart stops beating, or a person stops breathing, this whole process stops. No

oxygen is taken into the body, and the blood
30 doesn't move through the arteries. CPR can
start the process moving again.

There are several situations where CPR is
needed. It can be used when a person has a heart
attack and the heart stops. A heart attack occurs
35 when the heart cannot get enough oxygen. This
usually happens because one of the two arteries
to the heart has become narrow or completely
blocked. The heart muscle cells that are supplied
with oxygen by that artery die because they stop
40 receiving oxygen.

One of the symptoms of a heart attack is a
feeling of pressure and tightness or aching in the
center of the chest. It lasts longer than two
minutes, and it may come and go. The person
45 having a heart attack may also start sweating,
feel weak, be short of breath, and feel like vomiting. However, there may be no symptoms at all;
the heart may stop suddenly, and the person
stops breathing. If CPR is started immediately,
50 it may bring the person back to life.

Electric shock is another situation where
CPR can be used. If enough electricity enters the
body, the person dies immediately. CPR can resuscitate the person. An electric shock usually
55 happens to someone who has been working care-
lessly with electricity. It can also be caused if
lightning strikes a person.

A third situation is drowning, or dying in
water, which happens most often in the summer
60 when many people go swimming. Children can
also drown when they are left alone near a swimming pool. A person trained in CPR can help a
person start to breathe after clearing the water
out of the airway.

65 These are the three most common causes of
sudden death when CPR can be used. There are
others less common. Someone in a burning
building may breathe in too much smoke and not

get any oxygen into the lungs. Some people have
70 an intense reaction to certain drugs or to the
sting of a bee or some other insect, and the heart
and lungs stop functioning.

CPR is an example of first **aid**. An ordinary
person can take a first aid class and learn what
75 to do until the patient receives professional help.
This might mean helping someone until an
ambulance comes. Then professionals can use
their equipment to take charge of the patient. Or
it might mean giving first aid and then taking
80 the patient to a doctor. CPR can keep a person
alive until he or she reaches a hospital.

When you give CPR, you breathe directly
into the patient's mouth. Then you press on the
heart in the center of the chest. You continue
85 alternating these two actions.

CPR is easy to learn, but you shouldn't
learn it from a book. You should receive instruc-
tion in a class where you can practice in front of
the teacher until you do it correctly. As you
90 know, if the brain is without oxygen for four
minutes, there will be permanent brain damage.
It is necessary to start CPR immediately when a
person stops breathing, or as soon as possible.
You have to know how to do it quickly and well.

95 If someone in your family has heart trouble,
if you go swimming a lot, or if you plan to work
with electricity, you should learn CPR. In fact,
everyone should learn it, in case they ever need
it.

100 Where can you learn it? The Red Cross has
CPR classes, many hospitals teach it, and so do
some university student health centers. If there
are no classes where you live, ask the Red Cross
or a nearby hospital to organize a class.

105 CPR is worth learning. It can give you the
chance to save someone's life.

help

MEDICINE AND HEALTH

A. Vocabulary

resuscitation	located	pump	strike
sting	first aid	react	lung
breastbone	process	drown	function

1. The heart is directly behind the _____.
2. Village people often have to _____ water by hand.
3. Volcanoes are _____ in chains and clusters.
4. Hail and snow are formed by a similar _____.
5. A bee _____ is painful.
6. The _____ of the heart is to pump blood through the arteries.
7. Children should wear a life preserver when they are around water so they can't _____.
8. Anyone can learn to give _____. You don't have to be a doctor or nurse.
9. The *R* in CPR stands for _____.

B. Vocabulary

chest	so	in case	shock
lungs	breastbone	process	ambulance
take charge	strike	reaction	drown

1. The _____ are in the chest and _____ is the heart.
2. In baseball, if a player tries to hit the ball and misses it, it is called a _____ even though he didn't hit the ball.
3. An electric _____ can kill a person.
4. An _____ is used to take patients to a hospital.
5. A strong _____ to a drug can kill a person.
6. Edward volunteered to _____ of arranging food for the party.
7. Handwriting analysis is a _____ of studying handwriting in order to understand the person who wrote it.
8. You cannot save up sleep ahead of time _____ you need it later.

C. Vocabulary Review: Synonyms
Match the words that mean the same.

1. worth _____		a.	a lot
2. miserable _____		b.	blur
3. contagious _____		c.	teenager
4. a great deal _____		d.	catching
5. at times _____		e.	vision
6. nightmare _____		f.	forever
7. confused _____		g.	value
8. adolescent _____		h.	location
9. permanently _____		i.	painful
10. sore _____		j.	unhappy
11. dawn _____		k.	sometimes
12. position _____		l.	sunrise
		m.	mixed up
		n.	bad dream

D. True/False/No Information

_____ 1. *Resuscitation* is a medical word.

_____ 2. Sudden death can be cured only by using today's technology.

_____ 3. The arteries take carbon dioxide out of the lungs.

_____ 4. Carbon dioxide enters the lungs through the airways.

_____ 5. CPR can be used in cases of drowning.

_____ 6. CPR can help a person with sleep apnea.

_____ 7. A common situation when CPR is needed is with a reaction to an insect sting.

_____ 8. First aid is an example of CPR.

_____ 9. Everyone should get a book about CPR and learn how to do it.

_____ 10. You should call an ambulance before you start CPR.

E. Comprehension Questions

1. What is the function of the lungs?
2. What are the symptoms of a heart attack?
3. What are the three most common situations where CPR is needed?

4. What is first aid?
5. How can CPR prevent brain damage?
6. What professionals work with patients?

F. Main Idea

What is the main idea of these paragraphs?

1. 2 (lines 7–14)
2. 11 (lines 82–85)
3. 12 (lines 86–94)

WORD STUDY

A. Word Study

	Verb	Noun	Adjective	Adverb
1.	resuscitate	resuscitation		
2.	locate	location		
3.	react	reaction		
4.	drown	drowning		
5.		similarity	(dis)similar	(dis)similarly
6.	relate	relation(ship) relative	relative (un)related	relatively
7.	medicate	medicine	medical	medically
8.	die	death	dead	
9.	light lighten	lightning	light	
10.	tighten	tightness	tight	tightly

1. With CPR, you may be able to _____ someone.
2a. The newspaper gave the time and _____ of the university entrance exam.
2b. The Chemistry Building is _____ next to the Physics Building.
3a. How would you _____ if you saw someone drowning?
3b. There are machines to test your _____ time when you are driving.
4. There were two cases of _____ at the beach near our home last year.
5. What is the _____ between snow and hail?
6a. What is the _____ between changes in the family and population growth?
6b. Population growth in industrial countries is _____ slow.
6c. Munir is _____ to the Minister of Education.
7. Jane wants to go to _____ college and become a doctor.
8. A heart attack doesn't always cause _____.
9. Before it started to rain, there was a lot of thunder and _____.
10. The little boy held _____ to his father's hand.

B. Compound Words and Two-Word Verbs

Make a compound word by joining a word from the first column with one from the second column. More than one answer is correct for several of the words. Some of these are also written separately as two-word verbs.

1. break	a. in	_____
2. stand	b. down	_____
3. work	c. work	_____
4. check	d. mate	_____
5. sun	e. rise	_____
6. home	f. night	_____
7. sleep	g. by	_____
8. out	h. grow	_____
9. life	i. walk	_____
10. over	j. way	_____
11. air	k. time	_____
12. room	l. out	_____

C. Summarizing

Write a summary of the text for this lesson. Write only the important information using three to five sentences.

D. Prepositions and Two-Word Verbs

1. Some children are afraid of the dark, but they grow_____ _____ it.
2. CPR stands _____ cardiopulmonary resuscitation.
3. CPR is a method _____ starting someone's lungs and heart again _____ they have stopped.
4. It is an amazing idea that there is a cure _____ sudden death.
5. You should take a class _____ CPR. Don't put it _____.
6. No oxygen is taken _____ the body, and the blood doesn't move _____ the arteries.
7. One _____ the symptoms _____ a heart attack is a feeling _____ pressure and tightness or aching _____the center _____ the chest.
8. CPR may bring the person back _____ life.
9. Then professionals can take charge _____ the patient.
10. Some people have an intense reaction _____ the sting _____ a bee.

E. Context Clues

1. A student with short purple hair walked into the classroom. Everyone **stared** at her.
   a. talked   b. swelled   c. looked intensely

2. I like your new shirt. It's very **attractive**.
   a. pretty   b. large   c. permanent

3. That young man looks **familiar**. I think he attended my high school.
   a. like a member of a family
   b. like someone I know
   c. like a relative of mine

4. Paulo was **confident** that he could save someone's life after he took a CPR class.
   a. sure   b. process   c. volunteer

BLUSHING AND SHYNESS

5

How do you feel when you realize you just gave a stupid answer in class? Or how would you feel if you were in the cafeteria, you dropped your dishes, and everyone **stared** at you when they heard the loud crash? You would feel embarrassed. When you are embarrassed, you want to sink through the floor so no one can see you.

looked intensely

If you are really unlucky, you also blush. Your face gets red as a beet, and you can't do anything about it. It seems to stay red forever. People stare at you even more, and you feel even more embarrassed.

Why do people blush? Not much research has been done on it. Psychologists say that people of all skin colors blush. Women blush more than men, and young people blush more than older people. Some people blush only a few seconds, but the blush can appear and disappear for five or ten minutes in other people. Usually only the face or upper part of the body blushes.

Blushing is related to general anxiety, when people feel worried and nervous about what is going to happen. Shy people blush because they are always worried about what others think of them. They don't have any confidence in themselves.

Shy people are anxious about themselves all the time. They can't think about other people's

241

feelings very much because they are too worried
30 about themselves and what others are thinking
about them. They think other people are more
intelligent and can do everything better. They
think other people are more **attractive** and   pretty, handsome
more popular. They believe others have more
35 knowledge. They become very shy if they have to
deal with people from a different social class, or
if they have to work with more intelligent or
more skilled people. Shy people get very anxious
when they don't know how to act in situations
40 that other people think are just ordinary. They
feel inferior and want to **get out of** the situa-   avoid, not do
tion.

Everything that shy people do with other
people is difficult for them. Two researchers
45 asked hundreds of men and women what made
them most anxious. They said going to a party
with strangers was the worst. That was even
worse than having to give a speech or have an
interview for a new job. They also felt unhappy
50 when people asked them **personal** questions in   about themselves
public or when they talked to someone in a
superior position. Young people were anxious
when they met the parents of a date. The first
day on a new job was also hard for shy people.
55 Shy people behave differently from more
confident people. They don't want to complain
about bad service in a store or restaurant. They
don't make suggestions or volunteer to do
things. They avoid social gatherings. They usu-
60 ally speak in a low voice.

Some shy people have physical reactions
when they have to face one of these situations.
Their hands get cold and moist or shaky, their
mouth gets dry, they break out in a cold sweat,
65 and their heart beats faster. They might have
"butterflies" in their stomach, or feel
nauseated.   feel like vomiting

There are three theories about why people are shy. One theory says that a person inherits shyness from the parents, that is, the person is born with this personality characteristic because the parents were shy. Another theory is that shy people never learned how to act with other people because no one ever taught them social skills. The third theory says that shy people learned to be shy when they were children because their parents didn't encourage them to be more confident. The parents probably comforted them and gave them extra attention when they acted shy, so the children learned that being shy was a good way to get extra love and attention. Now researchers say that apparently all three theories are true.

A study at Harvard University showed that even some **infants** acted shy when they were faced with something new and strange. They became silent and their heartbeat changed. Other infants were not afraid when faced with something **unfamiliar**, and their heartbeat didn't change. They appeared to have more confidence. This seems to prove that some of these infants inherited shyness; they didn't learn it.

These children were observed again when they were in kindergarten. None of the nonshy children had become shy. A few of the shy ones were less shy; apparently their parents had helped them learn to be more confident. Most of these children who had become more confident were boys.

Shy people have exaggerated feelings about themselves. They are very concerned about their outward behavior, their feelings of self-consciousness, and their physical symptoms of shyness. They are so anxious about themselves that the feelings of others don't touch them. They think everyone else is very self-confident. Obviously, no one is completely self-confident about their

babies

strange, unknown

knowledge and social skills and excellence at work. Everyone is shy in certain situations.

110   Can shy people change their behavior? Sometimes they can force themselves to do things that are difficult. "Practice makes perfect." If they practice enough, the difficult situations become easier. However, it takes a lot of
115 courage to do this.

People who have more self-confidence can notice when people are shy and encourage them to talk and praise them when they are successful in their job or studies. Shy people feel miserable
120 much of the time. Others can help them feel more comfortable.

A. Vocabulary

confidence	stupid	stare	blush
attractive	skilled	encouraged	infant
unfamiliar	inherited	personal	nausea

1. Shy people are afraid of new and _____ experiences.
2. Another word for *baby* is _____.
3. Is it impolite to ask someone _____ questions?
4. Some people _____ when they feel embarrassed.
5. _____ is a feeling that you want to vomit.
6. John's parents _____ him to stay in school even though his grades were not very good.
7. Mark _____ red hair from his mother.
8. It is impolite to _____ at people.
9. If you are sure of yourself, you have _____ in yourself.
10. No question is _____ if you learn something from it.
11. An electrician is a _____ worker.

B. Vocabulary

courage	suggestion	deal	complains
attractive	stare	service	get out of
exaggerated	anxiety	concerned	praised

1. Most television stars are _____.
2. Shy people suffer from _____ in their relations with other people.
3. Leila is _____ about her brother. He hasn't called her for three weeks.
4. A brave person has a lot of _____.
5. One of the students made a good _____ for the International Day program.
6. It is difficult to _____ with a child who doesn't behave well.
7. Mr. and Mrs. Miki _____ their son who had just won a prize for his research paper.
8. Tom said he earns $1000 every two weeks, but he is really paid only $800. He _____.
9. David always tries to _____ giving a speech in class because he is shy.
10. Ali always _____ that he has too much homework.
11. This restaurant has good food, but the _____ is slow.

C. Vocabulary Review
Match the words with the definitions.

1. nervous _____
2. period _____
3. habit _____
4. meanwhile _____
5. fever _____
6. pregnant _____
7. location _____
8. strike _____
9. react _____
10. drown _____
11. solar _____
12. observe _____

a. length of time
b. at the same time
c. stage
d. act in response to something
e. grind
f. hit
g. watch
h. die in water
i. anxious
j. usual action
k. high body temperature
l. of the sun
m. place
n. going to become a mother

D. True/False

_____ 1. *Blush* means about the same as *embarrassed*.

_____ 2. Young people blush more than old people.

_____ 3. Shy people don't have confidence in themselves.

_____ 4. Shy people worry about others because they think maybe they are shy too.

_____ 5. Nonshy people are usually more physically attractive than shy people.

_____ 6. For a shy person, giving a speech is sometimes worse than going to a party with strangers.

_____ 7. Nausea is a physical reaction.

_____ 8. It appears that some individuals learn to be shy as children.

_____ 9. Shy people can learn to have more confidence in themselves.

_____ 10. Shyness is inherited.

_____ 11. Most people never suffer from shyness.

E. Comprehension Questions

1. What happens when a person blushes?
2. Why does blushing make someone feel even more embarrassed?
3. Why don't shy people think about the feelings of others?
4. What do they think about others in comparison with themselves?
5. What did shy people say was the most difficult thing to do?
6. Which situation in paragraph 6 would make you the most anxious?
7. What are some physical conditions caused by shyness?
8. Why does the study of shy infants seem to prove that they inherited shyness?
9. Name two situations shy people would probably like to get out of.
10. Is it easy for a shy person to talk in class? Why?

F. Main Idea
What is the main idea of these paragraphs?

1. 4 (lines 21–26)
2. 5 (lines 27–42)
3. 6 (lines 43–54)
4. 10 (lines 84–92)

WORD STUDY

A. Word Forms

	Verb	Noun	Adjective	Adverb
1.		anxiety	anxious	anxiously
2.	encourage	encouragement	encouraged	
3.	discourage	discouragement	discouraged	
4.	confide	confidence	confident	confidently
5.	personalize	person	personal	personally
6.		stupidity	stupid	stupidly
7.	attract	attraction	(un)attractive	(un)attractively
8.	inherit	inheritance		
9.	familiarize	familiarity	(un)familiar	familiarly
10.	suggest	suggestion		
11.	complain	complaint		complainingly
12.	exaggerate	exaggeration		
13.	serve	service		

1. The students waited _____ to hear the results of the test.

2a. A shy child needs a lot of _____ to build self-confidence.

2b. Marie was _____ by the results of her physical exam after a long illness.

3. Michael felt _____ when he wasn't accepted at the university that was his first choice.

4. Joan stood _____ before the class and began her speech.

5a. If you tell the salesperson your initials, they will _____ your new suitcase at no extra charge.

5b. _____, I like my initials on my luggage.

6. Marie felt _____ because she did the exercise without reading the directions and did it all wrong.

7. Honey _____ flies and ants. Flies and ants are _____ by honey.

8. Tom _____ a small business and some money from his father when his father died. His friend received a large _____ from his favorite uncle.

9. If you _____ yourself with the language center before the first day of classes, you will not get confused about where you should go.

10. I _____ that we take a CPR class this month. That's a good
    _____.
11. If you have any _____ about the television set you bought,
    take it back to the store.
12. To say that you couldn't go to sleep at all last night is an _____.
    You are _____.
13. A waiter _____ food in a restaurant.

B. Irregular Verbs

Learn these verbs. Then put the right verb form in the blanks, using the first verb in the first sentence, and so on.

	Simple	**Past**	**Past Participle**
1.	tear	tore	torn
2.	light	lit or lighted	lit or lighted
3.	lie	lay	lain
4.	swell	swelled	swollen
5.	grind	ground	ground
6.	strike	struck	struck
7.	sting	stung	stung
8.	stick	stuck	stuck
9.	deal	dealt	dealt

1. Alice _____ her new blouse.
2. Dan _____ a fire in the living room fireplace.
3. In some countries, it is the custom to _____ down for a
   rest in the middle of the day.
4. Ms. Baxter's hand is _____ because she shut it in the car
   door.
5. Mr. Thomas _____ some fresh coffee beans and made
   coffee.
6. When the clock _____ twelve, the people in the street
   knew it was noon.
7. Bob got _____ by a bee.
8. The roadrunner _____ out its head in front when it runs.
9. Mr. Nevins is a car dealer. He _____ in new and used cars.

C. Two-Word Verbs: Review

1. Sixteen people showed _____ for volleyball practice.
2. Never put _____ until tomorrow what you can do today.
3. What time does your plane get _____?
4. Were you brought _____ in the city or country?
5. The teacher left _____ one student on the class list.
6. Do you dress _____ for dinner at an expensive restaurant?
7. Look _____! There's a hole in the sidewalk.
8. I have to read _____ _____ a subject for my speech.
9. Kim had _____ a warm jacket, so I knew it was cold outside.
10. The Bakers have to buy new shoes for the daughter. She grew _____ _____ her old ones.
11. We tried to get _____ _____ helping out our cousin, but we had to do it.

D. Missing Words
Fill in any word that is correct.

1. How _____ you feel if you were _____ _____ cafeteria, you dropped _____ dishes, _____ every stared _____ you when they heard ____ loud crash?
2. Your face _____ red and you can't do _____ about it.
3. No one _____ done much research _____ it.
4. _____ blush more than men, and _____ people blush more than _____ people.
5. Some people blush only _____ few seconds, but _____ blush can appear _____ disappear for five _____ ten minutes in other people.
6. One theory says that _____ shy person inherits shyness _____ the parent; that _____, the person _____ with this personality characteristic.
7. Another theory is _____ shy people never learned _____ to act ____ other people.

E. Context Clues

These words have more than one meaning. Choose the meaning of the words as they are used in these sentences.

1. Mr. Becker has worked in the **field** of computer science for 10 years.
   a. an area of specialization
   b. a place where animals or plants are raised
   c. the place where baseball is played

2. Leila is often late for class because she has to walk **so far** from her apartment.
   a. until now   b. such a long distance   c. far enough

3. There are 2.2 **pounds** in a kilo.
   a. the unit of English money
   b. hits or strikes
   c. a unit of weight

4. Trappers sometimes **cure** the skins of the animals they catch before they sell them.
   a. dry and prepare for use
   b. make better
   c. a kind of medicine

5. The **current** value of gold is $321.
   a. the movement of electricity
   b. at this time
   c. the movement of a stream of water in the ocean

6. I know that it isn't **so**.
   a. very   b. too   c. true

7. Ali and Muhammed live in a large apartment **complex** near the university.
   a. related group of buildings
   b. complicated
   c. anxiety

VOCABULARY

INDEX OF EXPLANATIONS
GRAMMAR AND WORD FORMS